Anna, you are a kindred spirit!

Carla Nicole

The Power Within

How to Heal, Love and Design the Life You Want

Carla Necole Williams

Names have been changed to protect the identities of individuals.

ISBN 978-0-692-43166-5

Book Consultant:
Shalena D.I.V.A. Broaster

Cover and Book Design by:
Theresa French

To Caedyn:

My favorite person

My best friend

My soul mate

My baby boy

Acknowledgments

First, and foremost, thank you for purchasing this book. It is my hope that within these pages you will learn to believe in yourself. Although I share stories of pain, poverty and fear, this book is about a journey to self-love. You can learn many lessons here, if you keep an open mind.

This is a book of possibility and hope. When I was growing up I thought the dysfunction in my family was normal, and in my community it was. I didn't get the love, affection or support that I wanted from my parents. I carried this emptiness into adulthood. I am proof that no matter where you come from, you can do and become anything.

I lifted myself out of an environment of fear and poverty by transcending fear and depression. I overcame the generational cycle of having low expectations for myself. I also learned that living in my purpose is not determined by a particular set of criteria. My goal in writing this book is to help you understand your own power.

I know without a doubt that we create our own lives. I've tested this theory out, and my truth is shared throughout "*The Power Within.*" This is empowering because it means you have total control of your life. If you don't like what you see, you only have to make a different choice. If you accept this with faith, you will see positive outcomes in your life.

You can live your life without self-imposed judgments and limitations. I will teach you how to operate from the spiritual dimension where all the depth is, your true reality. As a limitless being, the desire to be bigger and better is inherent in you. Your need to evolve and expand is intuitive. There's nothing wrong with wanting to be great. It is what you were born to be. And you will never be satisfied being less than what you are capable of being.

Empower yourself by learning to love, value and appreciate who you are. You are special and unlike any other person in this world. You have unique talents and gifts that can make this world a better place. You are perfect just as you are; flaws and all. You are already able and whole, and it's time you embraced your light. Truly know who you are. Your body, personality and spirit are the perfect expression of God. You're the trinity. There are so many layers to you other than what you see on the surface.

As a special gift, please be sure to claim your FREE *"Power Within"* Action guide! Click here to download it: http://carlanecolewilliams.com

Love,

Carla

P.S. Be sure to connect with me at the following places:
http://www.carlanecolewilliams.com
https://www.facebook.com/CarlaNecoleWilliams
https://twitter.com/carlanecolemba

"Our deepest fear is not that we are inadequate. Our deepest fear is that we are powerful beyond measure. It is our light, not our darkness that most frightens us. We ask ourselves, who am I to be brilliant, gorgeous, talented, and fabulous? Actually, who are you not to be? You are a child of God. Your playing small does not serve the world."

- Marianne Williamson

Table of Contents

Chapter 1

Meet Your Inner Child

"After awhile the middle-aged person who lives in her head begins to talk to her soul, the kid."

— Anne Lamott

Regardless of your age, you may have experienced several problems or heartaches in the past. Whether it was abuse, loneliness, insecurity, lack of attention or affection from your family or even bullying; all of these experiences have an effect upon your life. Most, if not all, of these sufferings and heartaches are not easily healed. And like any other human being, you likely carry the pain of the past into the present.

How do you treat yourself? I'm not talking about whether you get regular pedicures or wear the latest fashion trends. I want to know how you see, think or talk about yourself on a regular basis. When I was a little girl I got so caught up in how other people saw me or what they said about me, that eventually I joined in on the negativity. There were times I said hurtful things about myself out loud, but my inner dialogue was always set on self-destruction. I perpetuated a cycle of abuse. That's why I focus on healing and elevating the "selfs": self-esteem, self-image, self-perception, self-confidence, self-acceptance, self-worth and self-love.

One thing about being human is that you cannot see yourself unless you have a mirror. You may try to bury and ignore the dark, scary and painful experiences of your past because you want to forget the ugly parts. But until you look at yourself in a mirror to identify and ultimately heal these wounds, you will be unconsciously in a bondage.

The world around you is your mirror

The world around you is your mirror which means that what you see in your life is a reflection of you. This is called projecting. If you are unsatisfied with what you're seeing, then you have the power and the control to project something new. You make this change by healing your inner child; learning to love, value and appreciate yourself. This is the only way to truly be free from the shackles of your past. The root of whatever challenges you have in your life must be uncovered and dealt with.

Healing your inner child directly relates to healing your mind, body, and soul. You will discover or recover your 'selfs.' The selfs are integral to healing your inner child because any hang-ups you have about how you look, your ability to succeed or the amount of abundance you deserve, stem from your childhood almost 100% of the time.

So, who is your inner child? Your inner child is your friendly, joyful, playful, excitable, trusting and sensitive side. It is your emotional and feeling side. In your innocence as a child, you are naturally curious and intuitive without any thought of caution or fear. You were born fearless, but because of the things you saw, heard and experienced, you learned what to fear and how to fear. However, some of the things you were taught to fear were not to be feared. You were taught to suppress your natural gifts and talents by being told things like: "stop acting out, sit down or shut up." And when you shared that you wanted to be the next Oprah or Shakespeare, you were told to "be realistic or focus on getting a real job."

Over time, your natural light was dimmed by the very people you loved, trusted and wanted to impress—your parents and other caretakers. Because you were a child, you believed what they told you and you didn't want to let them down. You yearned for their acceptance and adopted *their* views as *your* own. This awareness isn't to be judged, but it is important that you become aware of the truth about who you are. Any disempowering or negative views you have of yourself are lies. By embracing your inner child, you will uncover some of the unconscious damage that you may or may not have been aware of over the years. It is possible to heal your inner child and accept that you are a good and beautiful person, inside and out. Although your beauty is different from anyone else's in this world; it's still beauty.

Repetition is the key to learning. As a matter of fact, that's how we learn to walk, talk, eat, bathe, and anything else we know how to do. It is through repetition that things are ingrained in your psyche. For instance, you don't wake up and consciously think about remembering how to walk. Walking is in your DNA now. You've learned invaluable habits through repetition, but you've also learned some self-damaging behaviors as well. If as a child, you were repeatedly reminded of your mistakes or how you'd let someone down because of bad behavior, then you may have started seeing yourself as a failure. Growing up doesn't automatically make the feeling go away unless you're aware of the lie and have healed it.

We are born with parents to teach us, guide us and protect us. However, many parents are fearful and dealing with their own guilt and shame which stems from negative experiences in their childhoods. My parents never gave positive reinforcement, showed emotion or said "I love you" during my childhood. As a result, I developed an attitude of: "I'm on my own." I felt very much alone. There was no nurturing or sense of safety. It is under these conditions that a naturally happy and adventurous child turns into a sad and distrusting one who ultimately becomes a sad and distrusting adult. The generational cycle of dysfunction continues.

What you experienced as a child relates to how you perceive and react to experiences as an adult. I had a client who didn't realize where her issues of neglect, abandonment and self-loathing stemmed from. Whenever romantic relationships ended badly for her, and they always ended badly, she would just "black out." Her definition of a black out was to do a Jasmine Sullivan or Carrie Underwood and bust all the windows out of her love interest's car and his house too, if she could get to it.

As we dug deeper into her history, she shared that she'd never met her father (abandonment issues), her mother was a crack addict and alcoholic (neglectful) and she chose the wrong men because she gravitated to those who showed her the slightest positive attention (low self-esteem and co-dependency issues). I helped her realize that she was holding on to a victim mentality because of her past experiences and that she wasn't loving herself because she identified herself as damaged goods.

You see, it's always more than just:

"I was abandoned."

You see, it's always more than just: "I was abandoned." Instead, we interpret that abandonment as "I'm not worthy to be loved if my own father didn't love me." It's more than just "I was neglected." Instead, we interpret the neglect as "I can't trust anyone because my own mother didn't see fit to care for me properly." It's not just, "I have low self-esteem." Instead, it's "I'm fat and ugly and no man could ever really like me." These are all lies.

So, what is a victim mentality? It's when you think or feel that 'bad' things always happen to you. It's that constant "woe is me" talk, or always having a 'pity party.' A victim mentality is disempowering. It causes you to feel like your hardships are predestined or that you don't have any control to positively change things in your life. When you feel like a victim, you're not motivated to take positive action because you don't think it will make a difference. What's unfortunate about this state of mind is that you can become complacent and soon your life becomes a self-fulfilling prophecy of pain. It's as if trouble seeks you out and finds you. As I stated earlier, your life is a reflection of you. It's not surprising that you feel even more pitiful after having a pity party.

Discovering your inner child allows you to project awareness onto your experiences. This awareness affords you a happy and balanced life that you probably don't believe is possible because you've been let down so much. Awareness is synonymous to light and allows you to see things from a different point of view. Now, not only can you heal old wounds, but you can get the lesson from them as well. Yes, there is a lesson in every pain because nothing you've ever experienced is irrelevant. We don't experience life in vain, although it sometimes feels like it. I want to help you to stop being a victim of circumstance and become a powerful controller of your own life. I want you to be the CEO of your life; the Chief Empowerment Officer. I want you to be free.

You can run, but you can't hide

I was the first person in my family to attend college. I even went to graduate school and obtained an MBA. That same year, I bought my first house at just 26 years old, which was a first for my family as well. Unlike my parents, all of my jobs had been "professional" meaning they weren't in warehouses or didn't require back-breaking labor. I'd changed the trajectory of my family through education and home ownership; however, I was still a product of my environment. The fear and poverty that I grew up with was still very much a part of my present lifestyle.

Until the age of 10, I grew up in the housing projects of Chattanooga, TN. They were called Boone Heights when I was a little girl, but the name was changed to Harriet Tubman as a measure to clean up its reputation and try to instill a positive image to the people who lived there. However, in 1985, when I was barely five years old, Boone Heights was notorious for drugs and violence. Even though it was scary on the streets, it was even scarier in my home due to my father's tyranny. My mother finally left him after over a decade of physical, mental, and emotional abuse. We escaped him by moving around the corner to live with my grandmother. From then on, we drifted from one ghetto to the next. Sometimes the places we stayed were worse than the projects because at least we always had lights and water in the projects. There were times we went months without lights or water because the grown-up's money went to drugs and alcohol. There were often 10-12 family members living in a two-bedroom, one-bath place. We were always crowded and there was zero privacy.

As a result I grew up thinking that life was hard and ugly. I believed that money was hard to come by, that there was never enough of it to get basic needs met and that people acted really ugly whenever money was involved. I saw people lie, cheat and steal money to satisfy drugs habits. I watched my granny beg for food credit to feed her grandkids. She was always in debt because she took on the heavy burden of caring for us. Poverty ultimately became an unconscious challenge in my life due to these experiences in my formative years.

Despite being highly educated, I never really believed I could make over a certain amount of money or deserved to live an affluent life like Oprah or Beyoncé. Even though I was smart, I downplayed my intelligence because of where I came from. After all, my high school wasn't exactly known for its stellar curriculum. Hell, we had gang-related riots in the hallways on the regular. Deep inside, I still didn't think I was smart enough to fit in with the big dogs at college. I didn't think I was creative enough to be noticed because I didn't play instruments, participate in dance or speak a foreign language like some of my peers from different backgrounds and cultures. I was insecure about my place in the world. Unconsciously, I convinced myself to just be happy that my utilities had never been shut off and that I'd done a better job than my parents had. Who was I to want more when I already had so much? I had such low expectations of myself, but I wasn't happy. This didn't sit well with me.

The ironic thing was I didn't have a whole lot. Poverty was like a shadow that I couldn't escape because it was part of my psyche. I thought that just because I "escaped my past" by moving away from home and never going back that I was done with the painful experiences of my past. I was not done with it though, nor was my past done with me. I had attracted the very thing I was running from: a poverty mindset. I extracted it and replaced it with an abundance mindset.

My baggage was my bondage. Just like the woman in Erykah Badu's song "*Bag Lady*"; my baggage was holding me back. This is how my poverty mindset manifested in my life: I got laid off twice in five years. In 2008 alone, I earned just over $6,000 (I thought it was $8000 until I got my latest social security statement). My house went into foreclosure. During this time I was working two, sometimes three jobs at a time and still had the lowest grossing year of my life. I was living off of unhealthy food like *Top Ramen* and sugary foods (just like as a child). My 'selfs' took another hit and would say to myself all the time, "I don't have what it takes." I was miserable and I was scared. I was also depressed.

At the time, I didn't realize that I had the power within me to get rid of my victim mentality. Yes, it was a victim mentality because I would think, "what's wrong with me (woe is me)," or "stuff like this only happens to me (I'm a weak victim)." I really believed this. I felt like nobody else in the world had it worse than me except for maybe starving children. But even that wasn't enough for me to pull myself up and be grateful for what I did have because these were just the symptoms of a larger problem.

Final Thoughts

Your limiting beliefs from childhood go much deeper than you think they do. They often become self-fulfilling prophecies because that's just how powerful your thoughts are. Emotionally susceptible children, which we all are, become dysfunctional adults. If you want ease and contentment, go back to the child and heal her.

Healing your inner child is a lot of work and the healing doesn't happen overnight. It's unreasonable to expect 20, 30, or 40 years of compounded pain to magically disappear. Not every part of your healing will be easy either, but the following steps will help you:

Earn her trust – She's been abandoned and on her own for a long time, so it's important to earn her trust. Imagine what it would take for you to trust someone who'd abandoned you. Remember, you are your inner child so seek to understand her issues of neglect, shame or guilt and handle her with kid gloves. Show her that you are there to protect, nurture and love her. Guide her with compassion and comfort her like you would a hurting and scared little girl, which she is.

Identify with her pain – Encourage your frightened inner child to have the strength and courage to face her fears and deal with them. It's scary and challenging to recall pain and fear that you've spent decades pushing back and trying to forget. Try to understand the grief and embrace it, rather than ignore it. You won't have to stay here long, you just have to project awareness here so that you can heal it.

Release your anger – It is natural and human to be angry as anger is just inverted fear. However, it is also important to transmute that anger into something positive so that it doesn't become who you are. You may not totally be at peace with some things and depending on how layered your pain is, achieving peace may take weeks, months or even years. It really depends

Transmutation = Alchemy

on you. Releasing anger is a gift you give yourself because you attract to you what you are. Purposely attract peace.

Remember you're not alone – Loneliness is the twin of a broken inner child. Make sure that she feels accepted and unconditionally loved. Tell her that she's not alone and how brave and courageous she is. Tell her that she's a survivor because she is. Reassure her that this is the beginning of a new and exciting life for her, where all her needs will be met and where she can thrive as her authentic self.

Help her to drive away guilt and shame and replace it with courage, love and acceptance because this is your true self. By embracing your true self, you will be embracing a new and exciting life with the wonder and awe of babies when they notice they have fingers for the first time.

Don't underestimate the power of healing your inner child. Healing her is the key to overcoming any negative thoughts and feelings that you have about yourself. You will experience how you were before your fears snuffed out your inner light. You will be reminded of your truths: You are limitless. You are unbreakable. You deserve abundance. You have what it takes. You are a good person. You are loveable. You are perfect, flaws and all.

To get more help with healing your inner child, download your free "*Power Within*" action guide. Go here to claim it: http://carlanecolewilliams.com.

Reflection

I see she uses alchemy as a metaphor.
I suppose loving yourself to light is a
metaphor. It's possible. It will happen
I love my little girl. We gonna make

it. All these doors to healing are ope-
nning me up. I need to take the advantage
of them. I'm being prepped for
something. I've found my Madison-
When I heal her, I'll be
under fear, false. I need to take
advantage of the time to heal.

Chapter 2

Understand Your Fears

"The cave you fear to enter holds the treasure that you seek." – *Joseph Campbell*

Do you ever get angry with people for little or no reason? That is your inner brat demanding attention. Do you ever get scared when things actually seem to be going *right* in your life? It is often your inner child who was often neglected or abandoned. Are you overly dramatic or freak out over small matters? Your inner child is suffering from the fear of not being able to cope at a young age to situations in your family that you had absolutely no control over. For example, if you had parents who shouted or fought all the time, you internalized those negative emotions with no way of fixing the problem. As a result, fear of losing control is often an inner child reaction.

What about romance? Do you mistake co-dependency for love? An example of this is making your partner out to be the father you never had or your knight in shining armor. However, the only thing you both end up doing is enabling the dysfunction of the other. Are you tight with money; yet, you still never quite have enough? Or is it that no matter how much you make, you want more and more and more? Maybe you binge-spend and a dollar is like fire in your pocket. Negative money habits are often an inner child reaction to money fears that were handed down from your parents.

All of the above examples have the same root cause: fear. Anger, anxiety, avoidance, co-dependency, greed, over-spending, procrastination are all just fear disguised and being called by another name. Remember, your current emotions and feelings are the driving force that creates what you will experience. For me, it was fear and distrust. Thus, I kept attracting similar experiences in my life.

The fact is that everybody has their own fears.

The fact is that everybody has their own fears. Fear is a series of physiological and chemical responses to a real or perceived danger. You may be dealing with some of them on a daily basis to some extent. You can immediately recall a time or times when you have been afraid. You have even placed an unconscious rating on your fears. For example, when was a time that your fear was a 1 on a scale of 10? Has there ever been a time that it was a 10? I experienced this extreme kind of fear.

When I was 26 years old I was the victim of a home invasion. I literally had a sawed-off shotgun pointed at my head. As I was lying face-down on the floor, I couldn't even squeeze out real tears. I was making the crying noises and movements, but it wasn't until after the perpetrators left and a friend hugged me that tears streamed down my cheeks. I really thought I was going to die. That was a real danger.

There's this acronym that I use to understand fear: false evidence appearing real. This type of fear comes from a *perceived* danger. It's not the type of fear that keeps you from walking down a dark alley alone or prevents you from walking in front of a moving car. Perceived dangers are often those that are invented in your mind and keep you stuck in a cycle of shame, guilt, fear, rejection, lack or any other low energy, low-vibration emotions. This type of fear holds you back and keeps you from realizing your full potential. Perceived fear keeps you from being great, which is what you were born to be.

Fear isn't all bad though. If we didn't have the ability to sense and react immediately to danger we wouldn't survive. When one of your five senses warns you that something is wrong, your need for self-preservation is engaged, and you take action in order to avoid danger or death. This is where fear is useful.

In actuality, the fears that originate from your inner child can also be useful. You see, we spend a lot of time and energy resisting our fears and running away from them, instead of overcoming and learning from them. But what you resist; persists. Whenever my clients work on fear, they realize that they've been suppressing and running away from their fears, yet the fears don't go anywhere. It reminds me of the saying, "You can run, but you can't hide."

Your fears that were caused by negative experiences from your childhood perpetuate themselves over and over, into adulthood until you heal them.

Earlier I shared how my father was physically abusive towards my mother for over a decade, which included all of my formative years. She once told me that he even beat her throughout her pregnancy with me, which also gave me the fear that I was unwanted or that somehow their fighting was my fault. Until I was ten years old, and my mom left him, I was a terrified witness of his rage against her. Whenever they would fight, I would be screaming, my mom would be screaming and my dad would be punching, dragging and kicking.

I was the "designated police caller." Although this designation wasn't official, it was understood. I called the police on my dad often. One fight in particular haunted me for many years, well into my adulthood. I was about six or seven years old, definitely younger than ten, and my parents had been arguing non-stop. I knew that my dad was about to hit my mom at any time, and she knew it too. As things escalated, she ran out of the housing project that we were living in at the time and didn't come back for a long time. I eventually fell asleep.

Well, sometime during the night she returned home and she got the beating that she had escaped earlier. Not only that, but this one was much worse than any of the other fights I ever remembered. As I walked down the stairs the next morning and wiped the sleep from my eyes, I didn't even recognize my own mother. Her face was a swollen, bloody mess and her body was so sore that she couldn't get up off the couch.

But worse than the sight of her, was what she said to me; "I called out for you and you didn't come." For years, I felt incredibly guilty because I felt like I let her down when she'd obviously needed me the most. Normally she could count on me because I was a very light sleeper and could hear a feather falling on carpet. I had trained myself to wake up at the slightest noise just in case I had to act fast! I always needed to be on alert at all times and ready to run to the phone before my dad had the chance to yank the cord from the wall.

It took me a long time to let go of the guilt from that night.

It took me a long time to let go of the guilt from that night, but it was replaced by resentment. I resented my mother for letting her little girl think she'd done such a bad thing. After all, she was a grown woman who could have left on her own. It took another few years for me to realize that my staying asleep that night protected me from seeing the worst beating my dad ever inflicted on my mom. I truly believe that my guardian angels and spirit guides were loving and protecting me that night, unlike my parents were at the time.

Because my father, the most important male figure in my life, was so mean and violent, I became afraid of all men. And it just seemed like I kept being victimized by them: a touch in a place that a little girl shouldn't have been touched by a grown man; sexually suggestive words that shouldn't have been said to a little girl by a grown man. Sure enough, negative experiences with men followed me into adulthood. As a freshman in college, I was almost date raped, and afterwards I was berated and called a tease. Although I knew the guy was in the wrong, I still found a way to blame myself, too; maybe he was right. I was in his room after all, right? What did I expect? My inner dialogue was eerily similar to the things I told myself as a kid. Somehow I had to break the cycle of victimization that felt so comfortable to me.

Some people have a hard time with taking responsibility for what happened to them in their childhood. And I agree that children are at the whim and mercy of their parents and other adults in authority. Therefore, I'm not asking you to take blame or feel guilty about anything that happened to you. I do believe; however, that we have free will even before birth. I believe that we choose our parents on the spiritual plane, and through our relationships, we learn karmic lessons.

Karmic lessons are traits that you need to learn in order to be balanced. They give more direction to your life, help you make sense of things that have happened to you and help you find your way through life. Have you ever found yourself repeating the same mistakes over and over? That's because you haven't learned the karmic lesson yet, and you will continue through this cycle until you do. Many people think of karma as a "that's what you get" punishment tool, but karmic lessons actually make us stronger as people.

So, it's not the child's fault that he or she was neglected; at least not on a conscious level. But I do know that karmic lessons are learned through challenging experiences. For instance, my karmic lessons revolve around the "selfs" that I mentioned earlier, and these in particular: self-esteem, self-confidence and self-worth. If I think back to all of the "iconic" moments that I remember, those three are at the core.

Final Thoughts

Wishing to be fearless in all aspects of life is unrealistic, but NOT being bound by your fears is very realistic. You can learn to overcome your fears by using them to elevate your conscious, versus living a life of restrictions and mediocrity. We attract the things to us that we think about the most, and if your thoughts constantly revolve around fear, then you will attract more reasons to be fearful. In "*Conversations with God*" Neale Donald Walsch writes:

> "Never resist anything. If you think that by your resistance you will eliminate it, think again. You only plant it more firmly in place. Have I not told you that all thought is creative?"

Although feeling fear is a part of human nature, enabling baseless fears will negatively affect your ability to make rational decisions and it will even affect your daily actions and habits. Baseless fear causes the destruction of your self-confidence and your spiritual and personal growth. It will also hinder you from living out your purpose because your daily actions and habits will be executed from a place of disempowerment versus empowerment. Regarding fear, in 2 Timothy 1:7, the Bible states: "For

God has not given us the spirit of fear; but of power, and of love, and of a sound mind."

An effective way of facing and overcoming your fear is by identifying the source, which are residual negative perceptions from your childhood. Through self-reflection and understanding the process of projection, you will be able to heal from the pain that you may or may not know that you have.

When it comes to coping with everyday fears, there are several things that you can do to keep them from having a lasting impact on your life:

Separate reality from perception - See the reality of the situation for what it is. Be rational and get clear on the facts. Soul search and explore your perception of the situation at hand. Ask yourself, "What's the worst that can happen?"

Identify your triggers - Isolate the specific aspects of the situation that trigger your fearful thoughts to identify the true source. When you change the way you perceive these triggers, you will learn to change the way you react.

Be observant - When you are being observant, you see things from a detached place. By becoming an observer of your fear, you're not in it, which limits impulsive and irrational action.

Think positively - Monitor your inner conversations and when you hear negative self-talk, stop and change the script to positive talk. Perception is a very powerful thing and how you feel about your situation dictates how you respond, so think positively.

Tune into your body - Be in tune with where your fear lives in your body. Is it your stomach? Is it in your chest? Use it as an indicator to tell you when something needs to be addressed. What you are aware of you can act on.

Remember to breathe - Because fear happens in the emotional part of the brain, it's natural to act instinctively. So when fear rises, break the fear cycle by stopping, creating space and breathing. This will give you time to calm down and give your rational brain enough time to catch up. This is where your breathing meditations come in handy.

Don't allow fear to stop you – Fear limits you. Don't let fear hold you back from living your life to its fullest potential.

To get more help with dealing with fear, download your free "*Power Within*" action guide. Go here to claim it: http://carlanecolewilliams.com.

Reflection

I keep fear in check, otherwise it will become a brutal taskmaster.
— I have a tendency to move forward fear that makes me brave.

Chapter 3

Forgive. Release. Be Free.

"You have the power to take away someone's happiness by refusing to forgive. That someone is you."

— Alan Cohen

Maybe you're still wondering why it's important that you be conscious of your inner child's presence. Essentially, your inner child is the aspect of your awareness that is naturally innocent, uncomplicated and carefree or playful. When you are aware of your inner child, you easily bond with the part of you that is pure Spirit. I honestly believe the reason children are so happy and trusting is because they're not that far removed from heaven. They still glow with the residue of unconditional love and pure light, which is Spirit.

For similar reasons, I also believe this is why children can wholeheartedly believe in magic. Tell a child who believes in Santa that he doesn't exist and that kid will go ballistic! For example, a colleague and I were discussing Santa Claus recently and whether children should be taught to believe in old Kris Kringle. We discussed how neither one of us ever believed in Santa Claus growing up because our parents didn't necessarily nurture that belief in us. And it wasn't because they were against the commercialization of Christmas, or because their religions didn't allow it, but because they were living out their own journeys which included drugs and alcohol not sleds and reindeer. To put it simply, the last thing they were concerned about was perpetuating a "myth."

But is Santa Claus a myth? That will be debatable as long as children are around, right? Personally, I do believe it's important for children to believe in Santa, the Easter Bunny, the Tooth Fairy and any other magical creature who brings them nothing but good things. I think it's important that they believe in magic and Santa Claus and anything that is synonymous with magic. I truly believe that if you believed in magic as a child, it's much easier for you to believe in spiritual things as an adult. After all, you can't see, touch, hear or smell Spirit, per se, but you know it's there. And when things are happening on the spiritual plane, what is that, if not magic? This reminds me of the following quote by Pierre Teilhard de Chardin: "We are not human beings having a spiritual experience. We are spiritual beings having a human experience."

For many years it was such a challenge for me to believe in God or have faith, because if it couldn't be proven with my five senses, then it didn't make sense. Thus, I considered myself a realist and considered my views as logical. I have a scientific mind, and no, I'm not a scientist or quantum physicist. I was just unable to let myself revel in the wonder of awe and magic, or in this case, spirituality. I couldn't connect with something I couldn't prove existed.

And believe me I tried! As a teenager, I was an avid churchgoer. Then in college, I got involved with a church that taught their way was the only way. Finally, after years of disappointment, pain, judgment and loss, I stopped trying to believe in spiritual matters, all together for quite some time.

It was my colleague who reminded me that the way I was presently living my life was defying my logical mind. I meditate to elevate my consciousness, I visualize in order to design my future with an empowered mindset and I've created a business based on my purpose. I'm consciously creating my life every day based solely on hope, faith and action. I'm rewriting my story and like magic it's unfolding right before my eyes.

I'm living proof that just because you didn't grow up believing in magic, it doesn't mean you can't recapture the innocence of your youth. I'd like to add here that I don't judge parents who don't allow Santa Claus in their homes. As in everything, this is a matter of perception and choice. I am saying that for me and my son, I don't see the harm in letting him believe in magic!

But what does Santa and magic have to do with forgiveness? As you heal your inner child, your spiritual freedom will improve and your emotional intelligence will be elevated. Both of these are needed for you to do the intense healing work called forgiveness.

Forgiving myself was and still is a huge transformative process in my life.

Forgiving myself was and still is a huge transformative process in my life. I literally had to go back and make things right with myself, the little girl from my childhood. From the time I was out of adolescence, I spent middle school, high school, college and a part of my 20's trying my best to forget about her. I thought she was ugly, weak, meek, poor, embarrassing, a coward and a crybaby to boot. Can you imagine saying any of these things to a child? It doesn't feel good, does it? But it shows exactly how low my self-esteem and self-image were. I had internalized everything that I'd picked up on, been called, seen or heard before and adopted it as my own idea. It was one of those, "if you can't beat'em, join'em" mentalities.

As I went through middle and high school, that pitiful little girl was everything I didn't want to be associated with, so I tried to forget her and repress any negative memories I had about her. It wasn't until I was lying on a therapist's couch some 20 years later that I realized what I had done. I had left that little girl behind and she was in a terrible place. She was all alone.

After realizing this and having a mini breakdown or breakthrough, depending on how you look at it, I felt the guilt, shame and pain of how little I thought of myself. I also felt bad for abandoning and neglecting a child who desperately wanted what all kids want, a little love and compassion. I had to go back and get her and most importantly, heal her. Now that I was at least aware of her, I had the power to change things.

Although my inner child had been forgotten, more like suppressed, she was still suffering. Yes, even though I was a 'grown up' now, I was still shackled by my past wounds and scars. I wasn't free. I realized that unconsciously, and sometimes even consciously, I was a willing victim of circumstance. I was letting life just happen to me instead of creating the life I wanted. I was disempowered by my victim mentality.

Throughout the years, I had gone through so much pain and lived in so much fear, that my emotions were out of whack, and I second guessed myself more than I trusted myself. As a matter of fact, my intuition rating was very low and I didn't trust that I could make smart decisions. So instead of choosing to live, I opted to just exist, and that perpetuated the cycle of dysfunction that I thought I had left behind. I didn't even know what I liked to do, so I didn't do much. I didn't know what made me happy, so I stayed depressed. I had no idea that happiness was a choice because if it was, then everybody would be happy, right? I didn't trust myself to have healthy relationships, so I stopped dating for a few years. Now that I look back, I refer to my 20's as my decade of depression. I didn't know that I could be alone, but not lonely.

In other words, I was comfortable living in my pain body. A pain body is the invisible threat of self-sabotage. And it is invisible simply because it is an unconscious pattern that repeats itself. The pain body is an unseen force that causes us to unconsciously seek pain over and over again. Of course no one would do this consciously. No one likes to suffer, right? And yet when you unconsciously create repetitive and unnecessary conflicts, you are finding some type of comfort from your pain body.

Living in misery had become a habit for me and I sang the "woe is me" song every day. I was not happy with one single area of my life, nothing gave me pleasure and I was out of balance. This showed up as depression, self-loathing, and hatred for others and society, and pity for myself. I was on my soapbox about how I'd been born a black woman, which is a double minority, and that any hardship I was suffering wasn't my fault! And because of something outside my control, "the man" was keeping me down and holding me back. I definitely was NOT taking responsibility for my life and was still identifying with my victim mentality and finding comfort in my pain body.

I was needlessly suffering because I had been holding a grudge against my inner child. A grudge that was petty, unfair and judgmental. I wasn't a scared and ugly crybaby anymore so what did I need her sticking around reminding me of my past for? But what I ran from just kept chasing me. I felt like I was trying to run away from my own shadow. It was pointless and my life was a reflection of that. I thought that I was healed from my past, but I was only in hiding.

How I healed her

I started to remember this little girl who was me. What did she look like? How did she feel about her life? It would have been good to have a picture, but I had thrown away my only newborn picture because I thought it was ugly. I thought I looked like a rat and I even proudly told this story as an adult. But now, I went back to those negative images I had of myself, and I reflected on those nasty words that I had said of myself, too. And I made a decision to not turn from my memories until I saw this little girl as the beautiful and courageous soul that she was.

At the advice of my therapist at the time, I wrote her a letter. I apologized to her for my judgments and my ignorance. Instead, I praised her for her courage and strength for not only surviving, but thriving in a situation that seemed hopeless. I hugged her and I kissed her and I told her how proud I was of her. I gave her comfort and talked to her in a loving way, as I would even a stranger's child who was broken and hurting. I realized that I wouldn't treat any child the way I treated that little girl who was me. Hell, I wouldn't treat a dog this way!

Most importantly, I didn't shame myself for how I'd treated her in the past. I just observed as someone on the outside looking in and I forgave myself. After all these years, I was finally able to show this little girl some compassion for living through a real-life nightmare. That little girl is brave. That little girl is a survivor. That little girl is me.

Forgiveness of self is one thing, but forgiving others is another ball game.

Forgiveness of self is one thing, but forgiving others is another ball game. When I think about my parents, I often say that I released the negative energy I associated with them. My parents were neglectful through indifference. My dad settled differences with his fists. Their God was crack cocaine and they had no idea how to love or nurture a child. They didn't know how to raise a little girl to feel good about herself because they didn't feel good about themselves. In a sense, I was just a casualty of their war. They weren't aware of the adverse effects that their energies would have on me. And if they could, I know, without a doubt, that they would give me a different story to tell.

None of that matters now anyway because I'm aware that we are all divine people, and our journeys are perfect. I used to hate the saying "everything happens for a reason." It's become one of those clichés that people use, but don't really practice. But now I understand. Had I not had the childhood that I did, I wouldn't have learned the karmic lessons that I've learned over these last few years. And until we learn, we will continue in whatever cycle we're in, and that's the truth.

Everything unfolds just as it should and the sooner you accept this, the sooner you can forgive and start writing your new story. It's the beginning of you changing the trajectory in your own life and family.

Not too long ago, I called and apologized to my dad because I had stopped speaking to him for a whole year. The fall-out isn't relevant now, but one day I realized the part I had in it. So I decided to practice what I preach and own my responsibility in the matter. I called him up and after the awkward greeting and pleasantries, I said, "Dad, I just want to apologize to you because I've been more concerned with being right, instead of being in harmony." Wow! Even I was impressed with my growth and maturity. He apologized, too, and we both felt better. Did it change the past? No. But it did create a space for a healthier, more respectful relationship from that day forward.

Everything is energy; our words, thoughts, emotions and actions. Even inanimate objects are energetic if you place them under a microscope. And because everything is energy, our thoughts, words, emotions and actions aren't null and void. They create something tangible and real. So forgiveness is really a release of negative energy on the spiritual and physical plane.

The truth is that we don't have the right to judge anyone, not even ourselves. I have learned to love my parents unconditionally, because we are all made perfect, yet we do imperfect things. It's called being human and it's what puts us all on an even playing field.

I can truly say that when I learned to stop judging myself, I was able to extend that same compassion to others, not just my parents. It's true that when you judge someone, you automatically judge yourself. When you judge someone else, you take away your own freedom to own up to a mistake and move on. So when you make the same, or a similar mistake, you feel ashamed and try to hide it, because if anyone found out about it you'd be "the hypocrite."

A judgment is just your perception of what is right or wrong and what's acceptable or not. Now I do believe in holding to your own standards, because they make you who you are, but I also believe in minding your own business. I tell people all the time, don't judge me for XYZ and I won't judge you for ABC. It is our right to live our lives how we choose to and that's what free will is all about. And just because someone isn't doing things your way, well, they're not supposed to.

There are seven billion people on this Earth, which means there are seven billion different ways to live life. So live yours the way you want to!

Final Thoughts

Judgment is an ignorance doctrine and I'll tell you why. We are all on the spiritual path and we are all at different places on that path. We may be in the same book, but we are on different pages and in different chapters. The learning is in the journey. Once you get to your destination, what else is there to learn? That's why as long as we live, we are learning and growing and elevating ourselves.

To stay stagnant is to die, whether that's spiritually or physically.

This realization helped me see that my dad's true self is not the monster I grew up with. His soul is as divine and pure as that of his inner child's. He, too, needs to heal his inner child, but that is for him to do, I cannot do it for him. We have to do our own work.

Likewise, my mother's authentic self is not that of a woman who is indifferent to her daughter who tried to kill herself as a little girl. Her soul is as divine and pure as her inner child's. Healing her is for her to do as well.

What I can do is love and accept them for who they are, for compassion is the opposite of judgment. I don't condone their past actions because we all have free will to make our own decisions; however, I am able to observe rather than judge them. I understand how they internalized their self-hate and pain and how it manifested into violence and abuse. I understand because I've been there myself. I've dealt with similar issues; however, I expressed them differently. This reminds me of Eckhart Tolle's quote: "To judge another by their outside appearance is a form of violence against them."

As I became more spiritually conscious, I also realized that my parents had some volatile and conflicting karmic energy that ran as deep and wide as the Red Sea, and only they could fix it. This is usually the case for people who find it hard to break away from an abusive or co-dependent relationship. I've learned that not everything is just black or white, and there are degrees of separation for overcoming every adversity.

I was able to see all these truths through love and forgiveness. I know that forgiving is one of the hardest things to do, especially if some of your experiences have been nothing less than horrific. I hope that the following tips will help you on your journey of forgiveness:

Change how you perceive a painful experience – Your feelings are the result of what you tell yourself about what happened. It's your thinking that causing you pain. You're no longer that child (physically) that you were when you were at the mercy of someone else. Take ownership of your feelings and figure out what it's really trying to show you. Your feelings are usually related to what you feel about yourself deep down. Is your, "I'm not good enough" radar going off?

Learn the art of observation – Notice your thoughts without getting caught up in them. Don't try to push them away, just take notice without judgment, by acting as a bystander. Feel powerful in knowing that you are the creator of your feelings. By not judging or blaming your feelings on anyone else, your sense of self-worth will get stronger.

Forgiveness is realizing that there's nothing to forgive – We are all either trying to, failing at, or succeeding in loving ourselves unconditionally. And everyone, in their own unique way, is doing the best they can. Once you are aware of how you have acted from the insecurity of your personality, you will have compassion for others who are expressing their insecurities in different ways than you. You can see the innocence in their behavior when you can see it in your own. Once you get this, you'll understand how every misguided action is a futile attempt to find security, love and freedom.

To get more help with forgiveness, download your free "*Power Within*" action guide. Go here to claim it: http://carlanecolewilliams.com.

Reflection

Chapter 4

A New Perspective

"For things to reveal themselves to us, we need to be ready to abandon our views about them."

— Thích Nhất Hạnh

Now that you've healed your inner child, it's time to meet the person you really are. When you ask yourself, "Who am I?" you're actually trying to figure out your authenticity as a unique person. Firstly, you're trying to find your place in the world and secondly, you're trying to find your purpose. Any ambiguity around these two things will cause you to feel a little uneasy about life. We all go through this phase because we are spirits having a human experience. It is natural for us to want to stretch, grow and see how far we can evolve in this lifetime. I call this the process of "Satisfying Your Seeker." And what are you seeking exactly? Why, more of your true self, of course.

In my early 20's, I dumped religion. I recently found an old journal from that time as I was capturing my thoughts for this book. I was going through a severe depression at the time, and a friend of mine bought me this beautiful brown leather journal with a strap. The pages are gilded with gold and it even has that little red string that holds your place for you. Well, as most people know, Healing Life Coaches usually coach people who are dealing with the same issues they've already dealt with. Most of the women I help are where I was 5-10 years ago. That's why I can relate so much to their pain and what they're going through.

As I was reading this journal, it was all about how horrible of a person I was. How I was undesirable to men, how I was ugly and unattractive and how I was obviously not worthy of love because I had somehow let God down and was being punished for the sin that I was born into. My attitude was that I deserved my punishment because I couldn't be perfect and kept "falling short" of the glory of God no matter how hard I tried. I shared with you earlier that for most of my life, it was hard for me to believe in God. I just couldn't reconcile a loving and just God with all the pain and disappointment that was not only in my life, but also in the world as a whole. But in my early 20's I was really trying to believe in something because I was so miserable and depressed that I tried anything just to feel better. In addition, I was still holding on to the "bible belt teachings" that "when life ain't going right, it's because you ain't right with God."

I carried this religious dogma with me for many years and eventually the load became too much to bear. I had to break away and I literally stripped down everything I'd been taught about God during my childhood. I discarded what I'd been told about his jealous vengeance, his harsh judgment, his wrathful retribution and his condemning me to hell if I didn't get my stuff together. I stopped believing in it all. Yes, I asked myself periodically, "*But what if I'm wrong?*" And my answer always came back as, "*It's a risk I'm willing to take.*"

Of course, I got some backlash. "You're not supposed to question God!" "Everything happens for a reason." "I'm scared for your soul." These fear-based reactions were the main reason I was venturing out in the first place. I was daring to think for myself because I could no longer live under the heaviness of fear. I already thought that life was a random and meaningless mess, but I also I knew that it was important for me to live my life on my terms. I felt free to do what I wanted to do, how I wanted to do it and when I wanted to do it without any guilt, shame or judgment—not from any person and not from any God.

Now that I was brave enough to go my own way, I also took no prisoners.

Now that I was brave enough to go my own way, I also took no prisoners. So, when my friend and I were discussing my lack of belief one day, and she was judging my decision because she didn't want me to burn in hell, I reminded her that she lived her whole life in fear. Fear of not finding a good job, fear of not finding the right man, fear of not measuring up, fear of failure, fear of making mistakes and on and on. I explained to her that I knew this fear all too well myself, and I was now done with it.

I asked her where was her faith because it's the first thing people ask when things get tough. But no one was practicing faith because they didn't really believe the hype either; not deep down they didn't. But they were afraid to voice that, and my voicing it was making them feel uncomfortable. I looked all around me; to my family, friends and co-workers and I started noticing some things. They preached faith, but never really tested it out. They all went to church, but were no better off than I was. They believed, but were always still scared, which is a lack of faith. I knew that I was onto something.

I didn't know that I was on a spiritual journey to find who I really am. Quite honestly, I thought I had counted myself out, but again I was willing to risk it all. Over the next ten years or so, I tried out many other philosophies: atheism, agnosticism and existentialism. I don't think I liked one philosophy any more than the other, my beliefs were predicated on where I was mentally at the time and in relation to how I felt at the time. There was absolutely no one else in my life that believed as I did, but for the first time ever, my way was working for me.

I no longer feared going to hell, so death couldn't be used as a threat or punishment to me anymore. I stopped feeling like I was being judged all the time, which helped me shed some of the guilt and shame that I'd lived with since childhood. And, I made up my mind that it was up to me to make things happen for me or not. Somehow I knew that it was going to be my decisions, choices and actions that ultimately shaped my life. And this was before I'd even heard of the Law of Attraction or "*The Secret*", which basically teaches, "like attracts like" and the energy you put out in the world will come back to you. This was a huge revelation to uncover because I was just kind of flying by the seat of my pants, so to speak. The problem was I still didn't know how right I was, which meant, that I still didn't know how powerful I was. So I knew that I created my own life in theory, but I wasn't creating it from an empowered mindset. My life was nowhere near what I wanted it to be as far as finances, relationships, and overall fulfillment. But this was the first degree of separation. Although I was free from religious doctrines that no longer served me, I still didn't know who I was spiritually.

"*Conversations with God*" by Neale Donald Walsch, is my modern-day bible. Every time I read it, I feel like I'm getting the biggest hug ever from God. It's quite an experience and my mind, body and soul is filled with unconditional love every time I read it. The book came about when the author wrote an angry letter to God because his life was all screwed up. His relationships, his health, his sanity and his faith was "going to hell in a hand basket." He never, in a million years, thought he would be answered directly from "The Man Upstairs" himself, but that's exactly what happened.

Allow me to share the fundamental concepts of his now well-known book:

- All things are one. There is no polarity, no right or wrong, no disharmony, but only identity. All is one, and that one is love/light, light/love, the Infinite Creator.
- Souls reincarnate to eventually experience God realization.
- Feelings are more important as a source of guidance than intellect.

- We are not here to learn anything new but to remember what we already know.
- Physical reality is an illusion.
- One cannot understand one thing unless he or she understands its opposite.
- God is everything.
- God is self-experiential, in that it is the nature of the Universe to experience itself.
- God is not fear-inducing or vengeful, only our parental projections onto God are.
- Fear or love are the two basic alternative perspectives on life.
- Good and evil do not exist (as absolutes, but can exist in a different context and for different reasons).
- Reality is a representation created by will.
- Nobody knowingly desires evil.

So, who am I, and who are you?

So, who am I, and who are you? We are Spirits, in physical form. We are all one. We are all connected. We are all God. Now, me identifying myself as God took me a while to absorb and believe. You have to understand that I had gone years without entertaining the thought that there was a God. So once I did open up to spirituality, I was like "there's no way I'm God!" For one, that's too much of a responsibility, and two, that would mean I could do absolutely anything. Are you kidding me? Just stop right there.

That would mean that there are no income ceilings, no dreams are too big and nothing could ever really harm me. Then I took it a step further. That would mean that I'm omniscient, omnipotent and omnipresent, right? That would mean that I cannot be created nor can I be destroyed, right? My mind could not conceive of such a thing. Thank God for books that were written that speak my language!

By now, you must know that hanging with me requires thinking outside the box. After all, Neale isn't the first person that talked directly to God and wrote about it. It's been said that the Bible was written over a span of 1500 years, by forty different authors. Honestly, Neale isn't the first or last person to write these kind of things. He actually presents many philosophical ideas from former Eastern and Western thinkers like Socrates and Tao Te Ching and Alfred North Whitehead.

There is one central message consistently carried by all forty authors of the Bible: God is love.

Final Thoughts

I don't expect you to just take my word for any of this. Go out and see for yourself. You'll know what resonates with you and what doesn't. The beauty is that you have the power and authority to create your life around the ideals that work for you; without fear, without judgment and without condemnation.

Whether you're a Christian or an Atheist really doesn't matter to me or to God. My purpose is to introduce you to yourself. Whether you believe in Spirit, God, Soul or the Universe, is of no consequence to me and I sometimes use them interchangeably myself. Maybe you don't believe in any of this and that's okay, too. Just believe in yourself because you can attest that your experiences are real. So choose to experience yourself at a higher level than you ever have before. You have the power to do this inside of you.

I use God and Scripture in my personal and professional life because it's my background and those words are familiar to me. I don't advocate for any particular religion or lack thereof. I do however, advocate for spirituality because it is about loving without judgment of anyone or anything. My beliefs don't negate or conflict with any religion or philosophy; it actually solidifies who you already know yourself to be. Jesus was really telling us to wake up to ourselves; to the power that we have as sons and daughters of the Universe. As a matter of fact, every religion and spiritual philosophy has the same core message, and Eckhart Tolle blends these seamlessly in his book, "*The Power of Now*":

"All spiritual teachings originate from the same Source. In that sense, there is and always has been only one master, who manifests in many different forms. I am that master, and so are you, once you are able to access the Source within. And the way to it is through the inner body. Although all spiritual teachings originate from the same Source, once they become verbalized and written down they are obviously no more than collections of words — and a word is nothing but a signpost , as we talked about earlier. All such teachings are signposts pointing the way back to the Source."[1]

It's not enough to just say, "I have faith" if you are going to take contradictory action. Our actions have to correspond to our believing for faith to work. You strengthen your faith muscle like you strengthen any other muscle: you practice.

Here are some tips to practice faith:

Practice with someone you trust - Proverbs 27:17 reminds us that "as iron sharpens iron, one person sharpens another (TNIV)." So get a prayer partner or start a meditation group.

Practice what you learn – When you're faced with a dilemma, like a bill that needs to be paid, don't worry and get anxious. Expect your miracle and see what happens. Test what you're learning.

---

[1] Tolle, Eckhart (2010-10-06). The Power of Now: A Guide to Spiritual Enlightenment (pp. 110-111). New World Library. Kindle Edition.

Get a spiritual mentor - Getting guidance from people who've "been there before" helps you make sure that your spiritual journey doesn't turn into a case of "the blind leading the blind." A mentor will help you see possibilities for improvement that you didn't even know existed.

Reflection

Chapter 5

Create. Design. Live.

"Life isn't about finding yourself.

Life is about creating yourself."

– George Bernard Shaw

People are under the impression that God wants or needs us to do anything for Her. This misconception is common because of God's reputation as this vengeful, angry and jealous entity that will let you go to hell if you don't obey Him. This just isn't true. Since God is powerful, don't you think that It can make you obey if It wanted to? Your role as a human being is to experience life and everything that comes with those experiences. The power is given to you to create your life in the form of free will. You are in control, which is a gift that was given to you for being courageous enough to take on the human experience. God is everything, and is in everything; thus, I use different adjectives (he, she, it) to communicate the truth. When we can speak about the Universe in a way that makes sense to us, we are free to live and express ourselves without fear.

The concept of free will used to confuse me to no end. I would say, "*Okay, if I have free will, then why will I be punished for exercising that free will?*"

The moment you are forced or coerced to do anything, you no longer have free will, and fear or retribution is an enforcer.

To me this was a lose/lose situation. Another thing that confused me was the belief that we are sinners from birth. Again, why should I be punished for something that's out of my control? I would think, *"I don't have a snowball's chance in hell if I'm born into the very thing I should be avoiding!" "Why does life have to be so hard?" "Why is doing the right thing so much harder than doing the wrong thing?"* But what makes something good or bad or right or wrong? The answer is, your perception of that thing. When I started thinking about things with a new frame of mind, they didn't make much sense.

We as Spirits, who are living on the physical plane as human beings, are here to experience every facet of life. And we all experience the ups and downs, highs and lows and valleys and peaks at some point. It is through these different experiences that we learn to express who we really are and ourselves. We learn what we are made of. You can't know good if you've never known bad. You don't know happiness unless you've ever been sad. Unlike any other creature alive, we have the power to create new experiences for our lives. Knowing and understanding this opened me up to a brand new way of thinking. I now had a different way of dealing with life. And when I started applying what I was learning, for the first time ever, I knew myself, to be a created creator.

I'd never really thought of myself as creative before because I thought creative people were the poets, painters or sculptors like Michelangelo or Da Vinci. Or modern entertainers like Beyoncé or the late Michael Jackson. I pretty much considered myself a self-proclaimed and very proud boring person. I'm a home-body, I can sit on a couch all day and read and I can stay inside for weeks at a time if I have to. Starting and finishing a book is my idea of a productive day and I've always been this way. I'm not naturally athletic and any athleticism on my part is contrived. I avoid it at all costs, although I could stand to move my body a little more. A lot of people would say I'm lazy, but why do I care about what they think? I used to feel guilty about it though until I learned how awesome I am. My personality, quirks, and nuances are mine and nobody else's. The differences that make me who I am are perfect and if we were all the same, life would be so boring. I've learned how to take those things that I used to see as negatives about me and turned them into positives. Now, that's how you empower yourself!

"*The Dark Side of the Light* Chasers" by Debbie Ford explains turning your negative traits into positive ones so much better than I do:

> "You're a bitch." My heart sank. How did she know? I knew I was a bitch, but I had been trying desperately to get rid of this part of myself. I had worked hard to be sweet and generous to compensate for this awful trait. Then dispassionately, Jan asked me why I hated this part of myself. Feeling small and stupid, I told her it was the part of me that caused me the most shame. I said that being a bitch had only brought myself and others pain. Then Jan said: "What you don't own, owns you."[2]

The point of my sharing this excerpt is that Jan helped Debbie see that she hated a part of herself. How can you love something that you hate about yourself? You can't. I believe that

---

[2] Ford, Deborah. (2010). The Dark Side of the Light Chasers. New York, NY: Riverhead Books.

every human being has the capacity for every characteristic trait, and the key to wholeness is embracing all your traits without judgment. Jan went on to give an example. She asked Debbie if there were contractors working on her house, (who she was paying lots of money) and she noticed them wasting time or doing something the wrong way, if being a bitch is beneficial? Of course, she said "yes!" That showed her that apparently being a bitch is sometimes necessary.

For me personally, if someone even attempted to harm my baby boy, all decorum is going out the door. You'd better believe that I will be a whole bitch, throwing a bitch fit of epic proportions. The moral of this story is the importance of you loving every part of yourself. It is another key to your creative freedom.

So, you say that you want a better life, huh?

So, you say that you want a better life, huh? Well, I'd like to talk to you about being in alignment. I'll be the first to say that I've accomplished a lot in my thirty plus years, but not all of it was true to who I was. In my defense, I didn't know who I was, so I was just going with the flow or blowing in the wind, depends on how you look at it. But when you know better, you do better. I also wanted to share what I know to help others do better, too. From this day forward, you will no longer have the excuse of not knowing.

When I was a little girl, I loved to read, more than anything else in the world. Now it's my second favorite thing to do, because now I'm a mommy to a gorgeous little boy. But when I say I loved to read, I mean I really loved to read. I would read any book I could get my hands on and when I'd read everything in the house, I would read portions of the newspaper, the backs of cereal boxes, the toothpaste tube and anything that had words on it. Although this may sound dramatic, it bears saying, "books saved my life sometimes." Then instead of just loving to read, I started reading to live.

Reading has served a great purpose in my life, and if I couldn't do anything else, I'd choose to read. When I was a little girl, I could always count on reading to take me to another place. Books were my escape. The characters and plots were not only exciting, but therapeutic for me as well. When I was reading, my mind wasn't on my present hardships, I was in another life. I found solace and safety in books. A lot of times, I found hope.

"All that book learnin'," as my granny used to say, paid off, too. I excelled in school, I mean I blew it out of the water. I was my high school graduating class' Valedictorian, and although I was an overachiever, I wasn't even competing for the top spot. I was just doing what I'd always done, making good grades in school. Then my guidance counselor called me into her office one day and told me that I had the highest GPA in my class, and that I needed to make A's from that point on to keep the top spot. At that point my academic competitiveness was kicked into overdrive, and I did it.

The ironic thing though, is the one time I had done something that would get my parent's attention, I didn't even tell them. For as long as I could remember, when I was old enough, I woke myself up for school, got dressed for school, came home from school and did my homework; all on my own accord. So I didn't think it would be a big deal to them. Besides, everyone knew that I was smart, so I didn't think they'd see this accomplishment as a big deal. It wasn't that much of a difference for me because I'd always been smart and school just came easy for me. Being smart became what I was known for.

But what I didn't know was that greatness was already at work within me. I know for a fact, that being an avid reader has helped me excel all my life, from elementary until graduate school. I never really had to study until I went to college and that was an eye-opener.

I went on to college, graduated and started working in my first professional job in the criminal justice field. Within a few months, I started feeling bored and blasé about work, but I stuck with it for almost five years. I was still under the impression that I could work my way to the top of someone else's corporation. My insecurities about my place in the world was intensifying and I knew that I wanted to do something else, to be more, but I didn't know what that more was. What I did know, was that I was educated, working and unhappy. So when I started feeling restless at my job, I did the only thing I knew to do; I went back to school and got my MBA. I thought for sure that more education would equal more money, a better quality of life and happiness.

Here I was living paycheck to paycheck, in a 'working poor' income bracket and feeling horrible about myself.

Here I was living paycheck to paycheck, in a "working poor" income bracket and feeling horrible about myself. I still didn't know how I fit in the world just yet, or where I'd end up when it was all said and done, but I figured I was on the right path. Getting educated is what I was taught to get ahead and the only "sage" advice my mom ever gave me besides "don't get pregnant or your life will be over." So even though I hated school, I went back because it's what I was good at.

I got my MBA and guess what? My finances didn't change at all, but I did take a huge risk. I quit my job anyway and embarked on my first entrepreneurial journey: an online eBay store. I bought a business license, a brand new digital camera, and a life-sized mannequin. I already had a computer. I named my business Vintage Riche and started going to consignment shops, thrift stores and estate sales. One of my most unique pieces was a chinchilla scarf with the heads of the chinchilla attached. It was an authentic vintage piece that I'd bought from an estate sale in an affluent part of my city. I was now an online vintage store owner and finally on my way to living the America Dream! Or so I thought. Long story short, I sold one pair of vintage flats for $3.00 (the highest bid) and I had to pay to ship them. In hindsight, I should have just kept the shoes for myself because they were super cute and I haven't seen a pair like them since. Needless to say, I didn't make a profit and I actually lost more money. I had to find another job.

Over the next few years, I worked odd jobs, sometimes two and three at a time to make ends meet. I also went back to school, but this time it was to get a technical license. I went to beauty school and got my Aesthetician's license, and I admit I really had fun there. I realized that my creativity was centered on pampering, luxury and making people feel good about themselves. It was truer to my inner spirit, too. When I would give a facial, the low lights, soft music and essential oils would put be me in a meditative state, and I was the one working. After graduating, again as one of the top in the class, I got a part-time, commission-based job at a local spa. I was still looking for supplemental work though, and after a few months of making virtually no money, I took a job making less than I was making from my first job that I'd originally quit.

In 2008 alone, I grossed just $6,000.

I had more letters behind my name, but I was still broke, and now owed even more student loan debt. Despite being smart and highly educated, I was still robbing Peter to pay Paul. But as smart and educated as I was, I'd been laid off twice in five years, and had to go through a government program to keep my house.

I was embarrassed and ashamed of myself because I was supposed to be the "golden child," remember? I was the girl who was voted "most likely to succeed" and the "person to watch" over the years. I felt like a failure. I just kept thinking "*maybe I don't have what it takes after all.*"

And I was scared to tell anyone my true feelings about things because a little black girl from the ghetto was supposed to be grateful for making it out, right? What the hell did I have to be ungrateful for? I should feel lucky because after all, I had my own house, wasn't on drugs, wasn't prostituting myself and I wasn't running around with a bunch of babies I couldn't feed. Hadn't I beaten the odds and bypassed some of the stereotypes that follow girls like me? Yes and yes, but I was still stuck in poverty and fear.

Now instead of being proud of my accomplishments, I resented them. I also conveniently forgot about all the fun I had in beauty school. I called myself stupid for quitting my first job to pursue a pipe dream. I pretty much regretted every decision I'd ever made. But, I learned two very valuable lessons: going to school wasn't going to solve my problems and I hated the very thought of working in Corporate America!

And yet, I was still putting in hundreds of resumes a month for corporate jobs. I didn't know what else to do! I did know that I wanted more out of life, and I thought chasing the almighty dollar would get me more out of life. And it's true that your quality of life will change with the more money you make, but that doesn't necessarily equate to happiness. I knew this on a certain level, but I was willing to work at jobs I hated to have more money. I didn't believe that I could have everything I wanted at the same time. I thought that I had to choose money and stress or poverty and stress and I decided on the former.

My whole life had been a financial struggle starting from the time I was living in the projects as a little girl. Money and resources were scarce growing up, and the grown-ups around me were always doing something ugly with theirs. Instead of paying bills, they were buying drugs and instead of buying food they were buying drugs. If something went missing in the house or somebody's money was stolen, it was to buy drugs. So I was resigned to the idea that having a lot of money would come at a high sacrifice. It was another risk I was willing to take. What's ironic is that my poverty mindset was so strong that I never got the chance to follow up on taking money and stress. I never got that corporate job making six figures, where I had to take work home, and sacrifice my health and happiness.

After sending out over 1,000 resumes and no one biting, I knew there had to be something else for me.

Final Thoughts

You've always had everything you need. If you didn't, you'd be dead. The universe has been giving you everything you want, in exactly the way you've asked for it. You've created every area of your life, whether you like it or not. You must take responsibility for this or continue the cycle of fear, poverty or whatever your cycle is.

Every experience starts with a thought.

If you want something different, then you have to think differently. A very crucial step in consciously creating your life starts with you taking full responsibility for your life right now.

This might not feel good, but it's the truth. And before you can even think about changing any situation in your life, you have to decide to: A) remain a victim of circumstance or B) break free from what's binding you.

I believe in you and created the space for you to tap into your own potential. But I can't do it for you. Dare to see things differently and you will see that there are endless possibilities for you. There are infinite opportunities just waiting on you to claim them. It is time for you to dream big, from a place of abundance and not of lack.

You are unstoppable and unbreakable or again, you'd be dead. Everything about you is profound and carefully chosen before you were even born. You were not created from an indifferent source who gives to some and not the other. Your nature is good and whole, so you were not born to live in mediocrity, broke or stuck in unhealthy situations. Your dreams matter! You matter!

"At first, you may only get fleeting glimpses of it, but through them you will begin to realize that you are not just a meaningless fragment in an alien universe, briefly suspended between birth and death, allowed a few short-lived pleasures followed by pain and ultimate annihilation. Underneath your outer form, you are connected with something so vast, so immeasurable and sacred, that it cannot be conceived or spoken of — yet I am speaking of it now. I am speaking of it not to give you something to believe in but to show you how you can know it for yourself."[3]

No matter what lies you've been telling yourself, here's the truth about you:

You are limitless - It is only the stories you tell yourself that prevent you from realizing your potential, and it is only your fear of letting go of these stories that prevents you from experiencing the life you were born for.

You are powerful - You are so powerful that your thoughts and spoken words turn into things. When God said that you were made in his image, this message was to be taken literally. And just as God spoke us into existence, you speak your reality into existence. So control your thoughts and choose your words wisely. You have the power to do so.

---

[3] Tolle, Eckhart (2010-10-06). The Power of Now: A Guide to Spiritual Enlightenment (pp. 110-111). New World Library. Kindle Edition.

You can do anything - If it wasn't for you, the world, as we know it would not exist, that's how purposeful you are. What you can do is limited only by the physical laws of the universe, and your own imaginations. We can't walk on water, but we have invented boats that can.

You are Spirit/God - You have been lied to about your true nature from family, society, and some religion. You are not evil, and you are not being punished for your mistakes. You are an amazing and wonderful being who has a right and a reason to be here. You are God.

Reflection

Chapter 6

Change Your Thoughts. Change Your Life.

"You will never be free until you free yourself

from the prison of your own false thoughts."

- Philip Arnold

Don't let your past experiences determine your present reality. Yes, I had legitimate reasons to be depressed, and I'm sure that you do, too. But what lessons did you learn? How can you become the victor versus the victim? You're the only one who can answer those questions. Yes, you! The answers are always inside you; never outside. I tell my clients all the time that I don't heal you. I just provide the space for you to heal yourself.

I suffered from depression when I didn't even know there was a name for it. All I knew was that I was sad all the time, scared all the time and I couldn't see things getting any better. I was just a kid, but I didn't know that there was a better way to live. Until I went to college, I thought all black little girls lived just like I did; poor and scared, all the time.

So, I decided that I was going to kill myself. Not only would the world be a better place without me, but I would also be free from fear, shame, pain and the dark cloud that followed me around. I would be free from the taunting, pitying looks and embarrassment over being poor. I wouldn't care about being ugly anymore and I wouldn't be around for anyone to laugh at my big lips or my buck teeth. I wouldn't be bullied or picked on at school anymore. I could stop worrying about my mom never coming back home because she'd been killed or overdosed somewhere. I wouldn't have to be scared of my dad when he was taken over by a moment of rage. And, I didn't care if I went straight to hell like I'd heard the preachers and other grown-ups say. I already lived there anyway.

I was so tired of being here. I was tired of life. I was ten.

Not only was I going to kill myself, I knew just how to do it. I planned my escape and I carried it out, too. It would be painless and quick. And I wasn't leaving a letter. I went in my mother's purse and took out her pill bottle. I think it was aspirin, the ones that were tiny and sweet. I knew from reading and watching TV that people overdosed on pills all the time and it didn't hurt. So when I saw that the bottle was almost full, I remember thinking to myself, "*this should be enough to get the job done.*" Then I swallowed every last one of them.

I got very sleepy, really fast, and I laid down to take what I thought was my last nap. For the first time, I didn't feel any fear. I felt at peace because all of the pain and sadness was about to end.

A few hours later, I woke up and I was mad as hell! Needless to say, a long nap was all I took. All I had for my troubles was a pounding headache that felt like my heart was beating in my head; I had a hangover. I was so mad at myself for failing at something that was so important to me. And I knew that I didn't have the courage to try it again, so I felt like a coward, too. I was even more upset with God because I felt like HE was keeping me alive to make me suffer more than I already was. If it was my life, then why couldn't I die if I wanted to? I was the one living in this hell hole. I realized there was no escaping. I spent a lot of time asking myself what I had done to deserve my life. That's when I figured out that it must be my destiny to live like I was. At least until I was old enough to live on my own.

I gave up hope that things would get better, and decided that if I had to wake up every morning, I'd just continue to do what I always did. Wake up scared, go to school scared, go back home scared and go to bed scared. Day in and day out I was afraid, but I learned to hold in my tears, hide my pain and act like everything was okay.

Ten years later I was professionally diagnosed as chronically depressed.

Ten years later I was professionally diagnosed as chronically depressed. By then I already knew I was depressed, but I didn't know how serious my case was. I'd lived and functioned in this space for so long that it became the norm for me. For instance, no matter how depressed I felt, I never let my grades drop all throughout school. Making good grades was my signature, so to speak, and I'd attached the very little self-esteem I had to doing just that. So when I stopped going to class, couldn't eat and wouldn't get out of the bed, my roommate knew something was wrong with me.

When I was a sophomore in college, I went to the funerals of three family members in four months. Honestly, I should have taken some time off from school, but there was nothing at home to make me feel better. I wasn't close with my mom, nor did I feel comfortable, or welcome, to cry on her shoulder. Same goes for my dad, nor did I even think of this option. So I went back to school, thinking that I could just fall back into my routine, but even my coping skills couldn't handle this pain. I was wrong because after that last funeral I was done for. To this day, I don't have the adequate words to describe my anguish. I felt like I was broken into a million little pieces, and I was suffering in a silence that was so loud it couldn't be ignored this time. I did nothing but force myself to sleep all day, every day, for about a week straight, until my roomie said, "Carla, before you do anything, will you please go talk to Dr. Brown?"

She saw me. For the first time, someone was trying to help me. Never in my entire life had anyone acknowledged my pain or depression. And here was this girl, like me, who had known me for less than a semester saying, "Can I help you?" I had been praying to die in my sleep because I didn't have the courage or the strength to kill myself, and I said "yes." I was willing to do anything for just a fraction of the load I was bearing to be lifted.

I dropped all but two of my classes. It was either that or get straight F's. Since my GPA was sacred to me, that decision was an easy one. In my mind, no matter what happened, I had to finish school and I had to finish on time. I was the "golden child", remember?

I made my first appointment with Dr. Brown who was a Psychologist and Professor, and the first thing she wanted to do was hospitalize me. There was absolutely no way I was documenting my condition to that extent. What would the people back home think? What would my fellow classmates think? I was not about to be the crazy girl on campus, or that crazy girl from Chattanooga who had to be medicated to keep from killing herself. I promised Dr. Brown that I wouldn't hurt myself, that I would take an anti-depressant and that I would keep our weekly sessions. She trusted me.

One of the first questions Dr. Brown asked me was, "What could I do to help you feel better?" I told her I just wanted her to make the pain go away. And it really was all that I wanted. I wanted some magical healing to happen, where she could just snap her fingers and I'd feel better. I wanted her to soothe me, be the balm to my Gilead. But, of course, healing doesn't happen that way. Since I couldn't be instantly healed, I wanted to just feel a little better, enough to get through the day and feel what was normal to me at the time. So we talked about me going to class to get back into my normal routine. I told her I was scared because I didn't think I could get through class without breaking down. Then everyone would be wondering why the hell I was crying and I would be embarrassed and pitied. She said to me, "So cry! With what you've been through it's normal for you to be sad." From that day on I went to class and I cried.

For the next six or seven years, I would periodically go to a therapist and take anti-depressants. Besides depression being a chemical imbalance, I had situational and episodic spells of depression as well. I didn't think I could get to a point of genuine happiness because I'd never been there before. My sadness had become somewhat of a habit and I didn't know how to break it.

I didn't know what I know now and that I was unconsciously manifesting more experiences to be depressed about. Now I realize the part I played in my future in the areas of my finances, self-image and romantic relationships. I reflected on my pain and anger a lot, even years after the fact, and found ways to be a victim over and over.

What you think and speak today will shape your future.

What you think and speak today will shape your future. What you feel on the inside will be created in your outer world. There's no way around it. My pain and anger turned into self-loathing and apathy and I was disgusted. I'd internalized my perceived injustices and became the judge. I started to believe that I was a failure and that I was defeated. I believed that I unlovable, unworthy and invisible. I was everything that I had been running from since I was a little girl. I was everything that I hated.

I stopped hoping for things to get better because I was conditioned for disappointment. I was always waiting for the other shoe to drop, so it always did. I stopped dreaming because I was plagued with thoughts of, *"But what if it doesn't happen?" "What if I'm not smart enough?" "What if people think I'm ugly?"* I felt like no matter how hard I tried or how much I accomplished, I still fell short somewhere. I didn't know how to make life work for me, but I saw other people doing it every day. Again I thought, *"This must be my destiny. I must not be destined to live the good life."*

It turns out I was great at manifesting experiences. The problem was that I was unconsciously manifesting the things that I didn't want. I had pulled myself up from my childhood, but it wasn't enough for me. Instead of focusing on what was positive in my life, I focused on what was wrong with it.

I sympathize with people going through depression because I know how it feels to hurt so bad that you want to die. I would like to share that it wasn't until I took action to heal that healing took place. Some of us need therapy, medication or both. And some of us just need to change our environment or to stretch ourselves to get unstuck. Wherever you are right now, just take action and watch what happens.

Final thoughts

The thief of joy is living in the past or living for the future. When we are depressed, part of our pain is because of our past memories and experiences. I know this firsthand as a survivor of a depression that spanned nearly 20 years. We have a tendency to believe the lies that we're told about ourselves, which cause us to perpetuate a cycle of self-abuse. You may unconsciously start to wonder, "Am I damaged goods because I was molested?" or "Am I unlovable because my father walked out?" Conversely, for people who live for the future, they start to wonder, "Will my life ever get better?" or "I gotta be in it to win it!" They think that they have to be in the rat race for any modicum of success. They are plagued with anxiety and totally missing out of the good that's going on around them in the present. Anxiety is just inverted depression.

In "The Power of Now", Eckhart Tolle writes:

"When you are on a journey, it is certainly helpful to know where you are going or at least the general direction in which you are moving, but don't forget: The only thing that is ultimately real about your journey is the step that you are taking at this moment. That's all there ever is."

Here are some tips for living in the now:

Stop worrying about your performance - Thinking too hard about what you're doing actually makes you do worse. No one's watching you, everyone is busy worrying about themselves. Let go and let yourself be in the moment.

Learn to savor – Savoring means to relish or luxuriate in whatever you're doing at the present moment. When you take a few minutes to actively savor something —eating a meal, drinking a cup of coffee, driving to work —you begin experiencing more positive emotions and fewer depressive symptoms.

Face your emotions instead of running from them - The mind's natural tendency is to attempt to avoid pain, whether it's painful thoughts or feelings. But in many cases, resistance only magnifies the pain. It's the NOT dealing with your emotions that keeps you in a cycle of pain. Accepting that there are some things outside your control relieves you of needless extra suffering.

Be an observer – Learn how to watch your thoughts, perceptions, and emotions pass through your mind without getting involved. Thoughts are just thoughts. You don't have to believe them and you don't have to do what they say.

Reflection

Chapter 7

Universe of Possibilities

"We all have two choices:

We can make a living or we can design a life."

– Jim Rohn

Tony was more like my brother than my cousin. Throughout childhood, we grew up in the same run-down houses, apartments, duplexes and projects. We grew up together through thick and thin and we had a special bond that was more like siblings than cousins. Being a boy, he was protective of the girls in the family, and I knew that I could rely on him for some type of security and safety. As we got older, he remained childlike in spirit, which really annoyed me. He was what you would call childish, but he was also incredibly talented and creative.

His type of creativity was bold and in your face. He could draw still photos of people, places and things. He even drew me once and how I wish that I still had that drawing. He could dance like Usher Raymond or Chris Brown, and he never had access to formal training or choreographers. He could do hair, too. I still have a picture of him combing his daughter's hair when she was about a year old. He was also a designer, not like Tom Ford, but he designed clothes and shoes in the form of drawings. His family, children and the women he loved were his muses. He would give them to us as gifts.

And when he was murdered, I felt like his life had been in vain. Hell, I felt like all life was lived in vain. I thought that his talents and gifts were wasted and I was angry that he didn't get the chance to live up to his potential. Instead of being on his way to stardom and millions, he was in the grave. Instead of living in the luxurious mansions of Beverly Hills, he never even made it out of the "hood." Honestly, I don't know if he even had aspirations of becoming rich and famous. I do know that he was just trying to survive and not become a male statistic of black on black crime. Yet he did anyway. I thought, *"What a waste of life!" "My brother didn't even make it to see thirty. He'll never see his son or daughter grow up."*

To make matters worse, he was killed in broad daylight on a playground while he had his one-year-old daughter with him. I had never been so angry and bitter before.

Instead of being this indifferent person I had become over time, I became this enraged and bitter bitch. I was like fuck justice. I want heads on stakes. I wanted bloody vengeance and more bodies put into their graves. I was about willing to sell my soul to the devil I didn't believe in, to meet out pain and suffering to my brother's killer. Hate consumed me.

"How could life have purpose when it could be snuffed out by somebody else in an instant? Why wasn't Tony given the chance to live up to his potential? If everything happens for a reason, what reason is there for a father to be killed in front of his child?" I asked myself all these questions and so many more.

And then there was the funeral. Now, here was this self-righteous pastor who didn't know Tony from Adam, talking about it being important to live right, lest ye burn in hell. I thought he was really audacious to stand up there and say that my brother was going to hell! How does that comfort the people who love him, we who really knew him? What was even sadder is that I probably was the only one in attendance who didn't believe that crap. Not because I was conscious or enlightened at the time, but because I just didn't believe the hype anymore.

So I tuned him out and decided not to listen to another word he said. But my baby sister was listening. She was sitting next to me crying loudly and shaking uncontrollably. She asked me if it was true that Tony was going to hell.

I didn't give a damn what this man was talking about, but I did care about what was being fed to my baby sister. I had enough sense to tell her to stop listening to him, too. I told her that she knew the truth in her heart because she knew Tony and the essence of who he was. Remember now, that I didn't know what I know today, but for some reason I felt very strongly that my message was right. To this day, she is the sibling whose spiritual philosophy is most similar to mine.

Tony's life did have purpose. Who am I or anyone else to take that away from another spirit? His contribution to this world was love and laughter. I've never met another soul like him and I'm willing to bet that my other family members feel the same. He was always smiling and laughing and he was so playful that it wouldn't have taken much for him to tap into his inner child. Like I said he was sometimes annoying, but in a good way.

Although I didn't believe in hell,
I didn't believe in heaven either.

Although I didn't believe in hell, I didn't believe in heaven either. I thought that when we died, that was it. It was over, finished, done. Ashes to ashes, dust to dust, we're no more. The end.

Then the next generation is born, they live, they die and the world goes on until humans destroy it. So while I knew in my heart that the people I loved weren't going to hell, I didn't have the comfort of thinking I'd be reunited with them in heaven. And that was okay with me because it was still better than thinking somebody I love was burning in a pit of fire for infinity.

What I know now is that condemning somebody to hell is another ignorance doctrine. Why would anyone go to hell because they think or act differently than you or I? People thought I was going to hell because I believed differently than they do. It's my choice and all a part of my free will. On a deeper soul level, everyone's purpose is different and every journey is unique. Our lives unfold just as they should. We were created to experience all of life, so why would we be punished for doing the very thing we were created to do? Even then that didn't make sense to me.

I still miss Tony and I smile when I think of him, which is often. I cry sometimes, too, because he's not here physically and I'm still human. Even knowing what I know, I wish that he hadn't left us so soon, which may be selfish on my part, but again I'm still human. The difference is that now I have comfort and peace around his death and I never ever, ever thought I'd be able to say that.

"*Your Soul's Plan*" by Robert Schwartz helped me to better understand the concept of pre-birth planning. This book tells the stories of ten individuals who, like you, planned before birth to experience great challenges. Working with four gifted mediums and channels, author Robert Schwartz discovers certain experiences they chose and what they wanted to learn from them. He records their actual pre-birth planning sessions where souls discuss their hopes for their upcoming lifetimes. In so doing, he opens a window to the spiritual side where we, as eternal beings, design both our trials and our potential triumphs.

The stories in this book cover challenges such as illness, the death of a loved one, accidents and coincidences. The book also explores being the parent of a handicapped child, deafness, blindness, drug addiction, and alcoholism from the perspective of pre-birth planning. The purpose of the book is the help you:

1. Understand how you as a soul create your life blueprint.
2. Consciously use your challenges to foster spiritual growth.

3. Understand that the people in your life, including your parents and children, are there at your request, motivated by their love for you to play roles that you scripted.
4. Replace anger, guilt, and blame with forgiveness, acceptance, and peace.
5. Deepen your appreciation of and gratitude for life as a soul-expanding, evolutionary process.

Final Thoughts

Since I've been there before, I know that sometimes it's easier to get dragged down by all the negativity and darkness in this world. I know how it is to feel like an ominous cloud is following you everywhere you go. All you have to do is turn on *CNN* or your local news station and you'll hear all about the economy, unemployment rates, terrorism and the high gas prices. And all of it will be negative and make you feel like crap. I could literally fill up this whole book with bad news, but I choose to empower you. Bad news is what makes headlines, but it doesn't have to headline your life. I choose to help you feel good about yourself. I choose to give you hope.

You are a unique interpretation of the universe and you have a right, and a reason to be here. You have unique qualities that no one else has and a lot of people need. You are not random, haphazard or produced from an indifferent source. Your very existence is full of purpose, wisdom and love. Everything about you is divinely profound: the way you walk, the way you talk, and the way you look to name a few. Your presence is a present, but what does that mean?

Your life is filled with endless possibilities. You just have to open your mind to see them. It's all about choice and you can choose to look on the bright side or the dark side of things. You can choose to consciously act or to react, or you can sit by and watch life pass you by. In everything, you have a choice. Are you going to be great or are you going to be mediocre? It's never too late to claim how powerful you are and make an empowered choice.

Here's the mindset you must adopt regarding the universe of possibilities that are available for you:

- There is a place for me in this world that is independent of my race, sex, beliefs, age, how I look or any other excuse I can come up with.
- I'm unstoppable because I create my life from the 4th dimension, the spiritual plane, where all my desires show up as reality.
- I matter and my dreams are valid the moment I dream them.
- I am perfect just as I am, flaws and all.
- I can and I will. I am enough. I am worthy. I deserve the desires of my heart.
- I am loved, loveable and loving.

Reflection

Chapter 8

Wealth Is For You

"The outer conditions of a person's life will always be found to reflect their inner beliefs."

~James Allen

I'm a certified Law of Attraction Wealth Practitioner, so I know a thing or two about an unhealthy wealth consciousness. If you've never heard the term before, wealth consciousness is simply the mental patterns you have around money that either keep you in a cycle of poverty or in a cycle of financial abundance. For instance, if you think that money is the root of all evil, then you probably don't earn a lot of money. Throughout this book, you've become more aware of how your thoughts manifest themselves. As humans, we have the capacity to make ourselves be right about things, so if you believe that money is evil, then you will avoid that evil. Think of someone who is a millionaire or billionaire today. Have you ever heard Oprah Winfrey say that her money is evil? The quickest way to gauge your wealth consciousness is to look at your bank account, assets, net worth or lack thereof. Another determinant of your wealth consciousness is how you feel about money and people who have money.

This is a snippet of a wealth consciousness session I had with a client:

Me: "When I say millionaire, who's the first person you think of?"

Client: "Donald Trump! The man is filthy rich."

Me: "Nobody can deny that Donald Trump is rich! What do you think about 'The Donald'?"

Client: "He's greedy, selfish and a cutthroat businessman. That man is the devil."

Me: "Oh, how do you know all this about him? Do you know someone he's done business with before?"

Client: "Nah, I just know that most rich people are like that. I mean, you can't have that much money without doing something immoral to get it."

So, what did I learn about this client:

- She believed in the "mo money, mo problems" motto – the root of all evil
- She thought that being rich was somehow dirty or unclean – filthy rich
- She thought of people with money as villainous – greedy, selfish, cutthroat
- She harshly judged people who are rich – increased money equals decreased morals

This client didn't realize that her wealth consciousness, or money mindset, was negative and disempowering. She realized that these thoughts and feelings had always been with her, and her financial situation started to make more sense. Her judgments and negativity around money was why she made just enough money to pay her bills and sustain herself. She had food, clothes and a car, but she wasn't able to do a lot of things that she wanted to do. For instance, she'd recently opted out of a group trip with some girlfriends because she 'didn't have the money' and 'couldn't afford it.' Most people have fallen on times like these, but she shared that she was a little resentful and jealous of all the fun that they had and she didn't. So she had all of her needs met, but her quality of life was lower than she would have liked. Honestly, who wants to live paycheck to paycheck?

Yes, our needs are important for our survival, but our desires are important for our soul. We are designed to want more out of life, especially if it's in alignment with our purpose.

Like my client, I used to have almost the exact same beliefs around money and the people who had a lot of it. But I made the decision to break away from my limiting beliefs and judgments around money. It was either that, or stay in the cycle of poverty that I had been in my entire life. I got certified as a Law of Attraction Wealth Practitioner by default in a way. I took the training to elevate my own wealth consciousness, and ended up with enough credentials to be certified myself. As I looked at my life and the lives of the people closest to me, I knew that conversations like these needed to be had. If we're not aware of our thoughts and feelings around wealth and financial abundance, how can we break the cycle?

I didn't think I was worthy of making a certain amount of money. Of course, I didn't know I had this hang-up until I started working on my wealth DNA. Just as your physical DNA is the carrier of your biological and genetic information, your wealth DNA is the carrier of your financial and abundance information. Your wealth DNA has been deeply ingrained in your psyche since you were a child it's part of who you are.

For example, I grew up in the projects and ghettos, nobody in my family was well-off and the adults weren't responsible for any money that they did have. Their money went to drugs and alcohol, and if you know anyone who is an addict, then you know how the addict is a slave to the addiction.

Even though my parents weren't smart with their money, honestly, they didn't have a lot of it anyway, and my wardrobe suffered a hit, too. I never wore name brand clothes or shoes, and with everything else going on, this lowered my already low self-esteem. Instead of wearing *Nike* or *Reebok* like some of the other kids, I wore *Pro Wings. Pro Wings* were $15 - $20 tennis shoes from *Payless*, which were basically the fake version of what everybody else was wearing.

Of course, as an adult, I know that clothes and shoes don't make the person, and we really do want our kids to focus on the right things. But as a child I didn't understand why I always had to wear *Pro Wings.* It was embarrassing back then and I got picked on for not wearing the latest. Just like it is today in impoverished communities, your clothes and shoes determine how poor you are.

It was common knowledge that my parents were on drugs and that my dad beat my mom, and my attire was just another thing to be ashamed of. Next up, our living conditions.

One summer, the lights and water were turned off for the whole three months that school was out. It was this summer that I'd rather been living back in the projects. At least lights and water were free! We burned candles at night and kept the windows open for breezes that never came. This is the South, after all, where summers are brutal. It was literally hotter in the house than it was outside. Every day we would walk a few miles to a spring to fill up water jugs to bring back home so that we would have something to drink.

We moved around a lot because we were always getting evicted. It was at this time in my life that I was the most angry and disgusted with my family and with my life. I openly hated my mother and subtlety hated my dad. I hadn't yet gone to college, so I was still very much afraid to disrespect him like I sometimes disrespected my mom. My parents weren't together anymore, and Mom was always around to get the brunt of my hatred. Inside, though, I blamed my dad more because whenever child support would catch up to him, he would quit his job so he didn't have to pay.

I couldn't understand why he didn't want to help take care of me. I internalized it as abandonment and a lack of love for me, which later turned into, "*I must not be worthy.*" This brings me to what I call a deserving set-point. Your deserving set-point, as it relates to money, has a direct relationship with your self-worth. When you have low self-esteem, you tend to think you don't deserve very much. Low self-worth is like a dreaded weed in a garden; if you don't uproot it while it's small it grows into an unruly mess. It gets out of control.

Low self-worth isn't just an issue for people who grew up like I did. Have you ever found yourself wondering why someone was so insecure when they seemed to have it all together? For instance, their family was supportive, money wasn't an issue for them and they were attractive and talented. It's because self-worth, or any of the 'selfs' for that matter, have nothing to do with outside factors. That's why even if you do find a temporary solution that makes you feel like you're "enough," the feeling doesn't last long, and you eventually move on to something else.

It was no wonder that despite my going to school over and over, getting a professional job and entering the world of home ownership, I was still stuck in a poverty mindset. My deserving set- point was very low and I had to find out why it was. Through self-reflection, asking myself the hard questions, meditating, reading, studying, hiring coaches, going to conferences and being honest with myself, I realized that I was allowing the painful memories of childhood poverty to affect my relationship with money. I was working, but not creating wealth.

You can transform your money mindset by elevating your self-worth.

You can transform your money mindset by elevating your self-worth. You have the absolute power to create a new and wealthy reality, but it's going to be an inside job. If you ask most people what they'd like more of they will say money, then turn around and say all of these negative things about money and people with lots of it. Saying one thing and doing another is the opposite of being in alignment with abundance. Although abundance isn't just about the money, finances are the easiest to measure in terms of being aware of where you are.

The thing about wealth consciousness is that it doesn't matter if you start with $1.00 or $100,000. You can either subtract from, or add to, those numbers depending on your money mindset. Everybody has a wealth consciousness financial blueprint, or as I like to call it a wealth-print, which is created by your deserving set- point or feelings of self-worth. A good example is when a person wins the lottery worth millions of dollars, only to be totally broke five years later. I remember about a single mother of six who won $10,000,000 (that's ten million dollars!!!) in the Ontario lottery, and had lost it all in less than a decade. She bought a mini mansion, drove fancy cars, wore *Gucci* and *Prada*, threw lavish parties, vacationed to exotic locations and loaned (gave handouts) to family and friends. Less than ten years later she was living in a rented house and riding the bus to a part-time job.

These types of cautionary tales abound, whether it's winning the lottery, signing a lucrative athletic contract, becoming an entertainment sensation or getting an inheritance. The money is not the problem, the money mindset is.

Wealth, without a healthy wealth consciousness, won't fundamentally change your sense of well-being.

Wealth, without a healthy wealth consciousness, won't fundamentally change your sense of well-being. If you're unhappy, not good at managing money and surrounded by people you don't trust, or don't lift you higher, then becoming an instant millionaire won't positively affect the other areas of your life. In other words, her windfall made the issues with money she already had more pronounced. Her deserving set-point was low.

On the other hand, there have been people who have made millions, lost it all, and made millions again. Take R&B singer Toni Braxton for instance. She's beautiful, talented and I've loved her music since she first hit the scene, but she has had some epic financial battles. She filed bankruptcy in 1998 and 2010, and in the latter, she was $50 million in debt. She owed a wide range of creditors and reportedly spent $2.5 million in hair, makeup and clothes alone in under two years. Long story short, she is now worth $10 million again. She went through tumultuous years with money and made millions back both times. Hopefully now, she has a healthier money mindset and will maintain her wealth.

Lastly, Donald Trump is notorious for his business bankruptcy woes. He's filed for corporate bankruptcy four time in 1991, 1992, 2004 and 2009, but has remained wealthy because he knows how to protect his personal finances. So although his corporations have filed for bankruptcy; Trump personally has not. Say what you will about 'The Donald,' but the man is smart about his money, and not only that, his deserving set-point is very high which is proven by his dominance within his industry.

Wealth and financial freedom are a far-off dream for many people because they don't think it can actually happen for them. I can relate to this because I was that girl saying, "*I could never make that much money*." Or, "*I'm not smart enough to make millions.*" I was that girl who used to think that people were predestined to be rich or poor.

However, none of that is true. In the twentieth century alone there was a boom of first-time millionaires, many of which did not come from family money, so you don't have to be born into a rich family. Being wealthy, for the most part, is a matter of mental attitude. If you're determined to become a millionaire, or even a "thousandaire", you will.

I had a client who was afraid that money would change her. At the time, she owned a business for six years, but never made any money in it. As a matter of fact, she was working another part-time job to pay her bills and was frantically looking for another one because she was barely keeping her head above water. When I asked her how much she'd like to earn in her business, she replied $30,000. I asked her why, and she said $30,000 would be enough for her to survive.

As we got into the dreaming part of our session, she shared how she envisioned shopping in Beverly Hills, taking a year to travel around the world, eat at fancy restaurants and do activities like horseback riding, because she loved horses. By the end of the session, I didn't even have to point out that she couldn't do any of that on a $30,000 salary. She soon realized she was selling herself short.

Awareness is the key agent in change, and in less than a year, this same client quit that part-time job, got into partnerships with some local businesses, hired an amazing team and started monetizing her business and started a TV show!

And she didn't turn evil.

From my experience, when people start making a lot of money, who they are is magnified. So, if you are selfish, then your selfishness could be magnified. However, if you are a generous person, your generosity will probably be magnified. If you feel like money will change you for worse, then it is your responsibility to find out which of your internal fears or character traits are resisting the idea of you being wealthy. Money takes on the energy that you give it.

Some people live their whole life never understanding that it is them who hold their destiny. You can change any situation or condition by deciding to become more than what you could be. Everyone has the ability to accumulate wealth, including you.

If you would like to be a millionaire, think like one. Think and grow rich.

Wealth is not a matter of luck, where some people catch all the breaks in life, and others catch none. There is no chance involved in financial freedom. You have to get in alignment with what you say you want and make your move. Everything will stay in its place unless you move it.

Final Thoughts

Money doesn't buy happiness. In fact, nothing buys happiness, because happiness comes from within. It's a choice. However, financial abundance makes your quality of life better. There is nothing noble about living without lights and water. There's nothing redeeming about not having enough to eat. There's nothing spiritual about living from paycheck to paycheck. Money can surely make life less stressful.

I've always known that I wanted money, and lots of it, even when I didn't know how to get it. Of course, there were people who were right there to remind me that "money doesn't buy happiness." And even then I would say, "*Well, I'd like to try it at least once.*"

We all know some brilliant poor people. You know, those people who can do great things if only they applied themselves or caught a break. Truth be told, talent is a very small percentage of success. For instance, do you know someone who isn't very good at what they do, but they make the most money in their industry or company? Again, only a small percentage of success is talent. These people soar because they believe they can.

We are all taught and conditioned in how to deal with money. Unfortunately, many of us were taught by people who didn't have any money or had a horrible relationship with money.

Your wealth-print is not just relegated to finances. Your deserving set-point affects your personal life, too. For example, women with low wealth-prints, usually attract men who have the same mindset. This way they can stay in their financial comfort zone and validate their wealth-print. Then they can say, "See, I told you I would never make that much." For years, I did this and attracted men with names like "free loader, moocher, opportunist, momma's boy, and broke." You get the picture, right?

Likewise, men can have low wealth-prints, too. These men will likely attract women who are good at spending and getting rid of all their money. This way they can stay in their financial comfort zone and validate their wealth-prints, too. That way they can say, "See, I told you women spend all my money."

When rewriting your money story, you must:

• Elevate your wealth consciousness by creating a healthy relationship with money.

• Make the decision to no longer be a mediocre earner.

• Drop your insecurities about, "Am I good enough to make this amount of money?"

• Stop sitting on the sidelines and put yourself in the game. Take action!

• Be around people who inspire and encourage your dreams.

• Realize that transforming your money story is spiritual.

• Learn to rely more on your intuition.

• Have faith that the Universe will provide your needs and desires.

• Work on yourself daily through meditation or other mindfulness activities.

Reflection

Chapter 9

Write Your Success Story

"There is no excuse not to be great."

– Steve Chandler

As children, we follow the footsteps of our parents, teachers and other important adults in our lives. As adults, we conform to societal ideals when choosing our mates, careers and even leisure. In every area of our lives, we are told to be realistic when choosing what path to take and which dream to dream. We operate by set boundaries and then wonder what's missing in our lives. What's missing in your life is more of you. It is now time to stop listening to all of the external voices, and listen to your inner voice.

What do *you* want? What are *your* dreams? Who do *you* want to be?

It's time to question and second-guess everything you've been taught, without the fear of judgment. To some people, questioning God is a sin punishable by death, but I did it anyway. You were created with a mind to think and a heart to feel, so why be afraid to use these gifts? If you do not challenge your most basic beliefs, you will continue to live your life how other people have designed it for you. And you will not grow as a spiritual being. Your life will continue to be the same ole same ole, and you will continue to live within a box.

Swim in unchartered waters, travel to unknown territories and walk into that space between your dreams. This is where you will find your purpose.

Fear will try to keep you in your comfort zone, like it probably has all your life. Only you have the power to overcome fear by facing it. No one is coming to save you. Nobody else can heal your pain. It is up to you to heal old wounds. It is up to you to fulfill your potential. You have to take responsibility for your own inner work. It is the key to the freedom that you seek. You are your own savior.

Know that no experience has been in vain. Everything that you've gone through can be used. Nothing goes to waste, if you choose for it to be so. You can believe you're a victim of circumstance, thinking that life just happens to you. Or you can empower yourself by writing a new story and making life work for you.

Most people won't test God, they won't test the universe, and seek their own truth. But you're not most people.

About 3 or 4 years ago I decided that I was going to try "just one more time." I had already overcome 20 years of chronic depression, been laid off twice in 5 years, almost lost my home to foreclosure and been in a series of unhealthy relationships. And I was pregnant with a child conceived in an unhealthy relationship.

I needed a change like I needed air, and, I needed it fast!

Yes, I didn't know how to make that change happen. The things that I thought would bring happiness or make my life better hadn't worked so far, and I was feeling defeated. I felt like a failure and now I was bringing a child into this world under less than desirable circumstances.

One day I was laying on the couch, which was pretty much all I did besides work, because I was eight months pregnant. I was 30 years old, and pregnant with a child whose father was in prison. I was a few weeks away from single motherhood, and I had all the fears of a first-time mother, and some. I decided that there was nothing I wouldn't do to provide for my son, but I wanted to do more than just provide. I wanted to thrive, but I had some form of contentment with my mediocre life because I was more comfortable in the pain I knew than to step into a new possibility. I was allowing the unknown to hold me hostage.

But now I had a kid to live for and the status quo no longer felt right to me.

I was still terrified because I'd always struggled financially. I was also worried about post-partum depression because I had a history of the mental disease. Plus, I just had to add in the "fat factor." I'd gone up and down with my weight since hitting puberty, and that was before getting pregnant.

I was thinking all of these disempowering thoughts when *Oprah's Life Class* came on, and she was telling her own story.

Oprah is a woman whom I admire and aspire to be like; she's one of my modern-day she-roes and she was talking, so I knew I needed to listen. She was talking about "*The Color Purple*" and how she'd never wanted anything as bad as she wanted to be a part in that movie. It was her iconic moment, her life-changing event. Here was this self-made billionaire saying how that experience meant more to her than her 25-year TV show, giving away her favorite things and becoming the first black female billionaire in America. The best thing that happened to her was getting to play the role of Sophia in "*The Color Purple*!"

When Oprah got the call from Steven Spielberg, the film's director, she was at the fat farm trying to get skinny. She thought that her weight was the reason her phone wasn't ringing for the part. And do you know what Steve told her? That if she lost a single pound, she would not get the part.

From what I now know, it was her commitment and intent that got her that part. She wanted it so bad that it had to come to her.

She was dropping dozens of wisdom gems on me that day and I felt my hope rising. There was this shift inside me, and it wasn't just a baby boy turning flips. In that moment, I knew that I could be great if I would just make the commitment to be great. That commitment included healing myself, growing into that greatness and practicing motivation and faith daily. My reality would catch up to me if I could stay the course.

As I rubbed my round belly, I thought to myself, "*Hmm, I think I can.*"

It was this new thought that set the wheels in motion for a spiritual journey that I could never have imagined.

I was the young woman who hadn't prayed in years because my prayers have never been answered anyway. I was the young woman who didn't believe in God because how could there be a loving God in this fucked up world? I was the young woman who dumped religion a long time ago because the doctrine I'd been taught made my fear worse. I was the young woman who thought that life was a random and meaningless mess, with no purpose to it. I was the young woman who thought I was born to suffer.

My outlook on life had been very bleak, but now I was starting to see things differently. I'd spent years stripping away everything that didn't fit into my life. I was shedding boundaries that no longer served me. I had to uproot the weeds of pain, anger and judgment to prepare a space of healing. I chose to reinvent myself from a place of power. I chose to write a new story to tell.

As you continue to write your new story, as you start to build your life from an empowered mindset, there are two things in particular that I want you to know. They will encourage you as your fears try to stop you and as your motivation wavers. You will question why you're working so hard to transform your mind and change your life, when not much seems to be happening.

You'll wonder "Is this doable, is this worth it?" The answer is "YES."

Anything your mind can conceive, you can achieve, within the natural laws of the universe. In other words, don't think you can fly and jump off of a building, because gravity is a natural law. But you can dream big for yourself; it's preferred. It takes just as much time to dream big as it does to dream small, so why not up the ante? You can have everything you want in every area of life. Being realistic is often just settling for less. You don't have to settle, test the universe in this. Wherever you see yourself in one, three, five, ten years and beyond, you are already that. You just have to catch up to your reality and working on yourself is what gets you there. This bears repeating because you'll forget: whatever greatness you imagine yourself to be, you are already that. You cannot realize anything that's not already inside you. You wouldn't know genius, beauty, impact or strength if you didn't already have those things inside you. "*Conversations with God: Book 1*" by Neale Donald Walsch explains this much better than I do.

It takes time for you to grow into your future self...

It takes time for you to grow into your future self. When things aren't moving fast enough for you, remember that there is space between the dream and the manifestation of the dream. That space is time, and it takes time, for some of your thoughts to become tangible. When you plant seeds, they don't sprout overnight. In this instance, your thoughts are the seeds. Give them time to grow. You may be a baby on your journey and you will need to be patient as you learn to sit up, crawl, walk and then run. But have faith that you will reap what you've sown, so plant the seeds that you want to see grow. Remember that no thought goes out into the universe null and void. You plant those seeds by transforming your mindset and taking intentional action.

Tools to heal and manifest

Over the years, I've tried many tools in the quest to heal myself as fast as possible. These are the easiest, and most common, practices that have helped and continue to help me. I know personally that these work, but it is up to you to decide which ones work for you. By now you know that I'm an advocate for creating your own way of living. You are different from anyone else in the world, so why wouldn't your process of evolving be different, too? With that being said, you decide how much time and how many days you should focus on any of these. You will probably even find some other healing practices that resonate more with you and that is okay. I will say that repetition is the key to learning anything, so please just practice something.

Trust that you'll figure out what serves your needs according to your personality, dreams and spirituality.

All spiritual teachings give us this seed of wisdom: "Ask and you shall receive, seek and you shall find."

Gratitude – Be responsible and take care of what you already have. You have everything you need to survive and thrive because it's already inside you. Show gratitude for the house, car, job, family, money, food that you have right now. Every person alive can find something to be grateful for. If you can't, then you're just not looking. Or maybe you're being stubborn and not acknowledging it. For some people, being negative is a habit that's hard to break away from. Being grateful for what surrounds you is the remedy for that. A good place to start is by listing five to ten things you are grateful for before bed each night. Smile as you remember them and your energy will instantly change.

Affirmations – Affirmations positive statements that replace negative self-talk. They are internal statements that are empowering versus disempowering. For instance, instead of saying "I'm a failure" you would say "I'm a success or I'm successful." If you have a hard time with affirmations at first, then instead of making a statement, turn your positive rebuttal into a question. For example, if "I'm successful" is just too much to internalize right now, say "Could I be successful?" What you're doing is questioning the lies that you or other people have been telling you about you. By asking the question, you shift your perception and automatically start thinking in a different way. Over time, your affirmations will overwrite any limiting and damaging beliefs you have about yourself or your ability to do something.

Visualizations – Use your imagination for the end you have in mind. Visualizing has been proven to produce what you desire to show up in your life. Simply have a very detailed daydream for a few and use all of your senses. Even if you don't see anything in your mind's eye, use your thoughts to be descriptive. I don't always see play by plays when I visualize, but I make sure the universe knows my intent by using my words, thoughts and feelings. You can also find visualizations on YouTube, where you're literally guided through the process.

Meditation – Another very spiritual practice is meditation. Since your healing, purpose and your truth are inside you have to go inward to find them. Different people have different experiences and I used to think I was doing something wrong because I wasn't having out of body experiences or profound visions. Meditation is simply getting quiet and listening for you inner voice and inner spirit guides. I think it's important to know what when meditating you will have thoughts, so don't think you're doing something wrong when you do. Let your thoughts pass through and refocus on your breathing or what-ever you're meditating on. As you practice more and more, you'll get better at staying focused. You can also find free guided meditations on YouTube.

Take action – As soon as you get an inkling of the direction that you want to travel, and you will, commit to yourself by creating an action plan. If you end up going in the wrong direction down the life, you will be redirected. When I first started my business, I thought I was just going to be an affiliate vendor for self-help products. I knew that I wanted to make a bigger impact, and on a global level, but I didn't think I was smart enough to create something that was original and transformative. As it turns out, I'm an original, and my business now focuses on healing, teaching, speaking and creating products around my purpose. I'm also an author!

I went from pushing other company's products to becoming the founder of my own company. The core of my business didn't change, my contribution to my business did. But none of this would have happened if I didn't take action. By taking action, I have like-minded business partners, I have a successful radio show and podcast and I no longer receive bank notices with negative balances. Remember that you have to set things in motion, or nothing will move.

Regarding this matter, W.H. Murray wrote:

"Until one is committed there is hesitancy, the chance to draw back, always ineffectiveness. Concerning all acts of initiative, there is one elementary truth, the ignorance of which kills countless ideas and splendid plans: that the moment one definitely commits oneself, the Providence moves too. All sorts of things occur to help one that would never otherwise have occurred. A whole stream of events issues from the decision, raising in one's favor all manner of unforeseen incidents and meetings and material assistance, which no man could have dreamt would come his way. Whatever you can do, or you can dream, begin it. Boldness has genius, power and magic in it."[4]

Release it – Expect your blessings, but don't become obsessed about them. Know that they are coming, however, remember that there is that thing called time. Spiritually things happen instantly, but physically natural laws have to be observed. As soon as you have a thought, the wheels of the universe start turning to make it happen, so don't be afraid to let it go. The universe never forgets the true desires of your hear. So trust and have faith that you are taken seriously. Just focus on working on you and remaining in alignment with what you dream. That is what makes things happen faster.

---

[4] Murray, William Hutchison (1951). The Scottish Himalayan Expedition. J.M. Dent & Co.

Final thoughts

Once you realize how much of a powerful creator you really are, you'll want to get started designing your better life. You'll be bolder with your dreams and your visions will get bigger. This is all very normal because as spiritual beings it is in our nature to want more of everything that's good. I'm a doer, and because I'm a doer, I have taken action when I probably shouldn't have. Because of my excitement and wanting things to "take off" I purchased some training and programs and hired some coaches that I wasn't necessarily ready for or even needed. I don't want you to do that.

Whenever you feel like the chicken with its head cut off, stop what you're doing, take a deep breath and go inside. Your intuition will tell you if it's the right move or not. Listen to it. I can tell you from personal experience that ignoring your truth will not benefit you. Yes, you'll still eventually get to where you want to be, but please take the path of least resistance. Following your dreams doesn't have to be hard. You will be stretched and challenged along the way, but you don't have to be stressed. You'll notice that when you're in the flow of ease, that is when things really start happening for you. Life being hard is just another lie you've been told. Remember, you transform your life by transforming your mind.

Robert Anthony states: "Action is vitally important but - it is not your action that makes things happen, it is your intent. You can reduce the need for action to a very minimum by allowing yourself to focus on what you desire until you feel the positive energy begin to move within you. This energy is not based on doubt, fear, anxiety, worry or need. If you focus on what you want instead of what you don't want, you will know when it is time to take action. And when you do, it will be effortless. Doors open and the entire universe will conspire to assist you in your desire."[5]

The following Tao quote reminds us: "When the student is ready, the teacher appears." Whether you know your purpose or not, just work on yourself. It's okay if you don't know exactly what you want, your answers will come. You won't be punished or left behind because you don't have it all figured out. A lot of life is illusions, smoke screens and lies, but your spirit always knows the truth. Your soul knows what's best for you and you do have angels and guides working in your favor. Ask them for guidance and help and it will be given. On this journey, you will truly have to practice faith.

There's no secret formula that's not available to you. Other people don't have something special that you're missing out on.

---

[5] Anthony, Robert. *The secret of doing without doing.* 1 Apr. 2015. <http://www.abundance-and-happiness.com/robert-anthony-the-secret-of-doing-without-doing.html >

And please stop thinking that something must be wrong with you. There's nothing wrong with you. You have what it takes to manifest your idea of success. You deserve to live abundantly in every area of life, abundance is your birthright. You deserve to be happy, and it was promised to you.

You always have the opportunity to reinvent yourself. You always have the opportunity to create your own way of life. You always have the opportunity to create the highest version of you.

You are ripe and ready to receive this message. You are ready to claim what's yours, which is why this book came into your awareness. Nothing happens by chance, your desires drew you here.

To delve more deeply into the concepts presented in this book, claim your FREE *"Power Within"* Action Guide! Click here: http://carlanecolewilliams.com.

Remember, there are no coincidences.

God bless!

P.S. Be sure to connect with me at the following places:
http://www.carlanecolewilliams.com
https://www.facebook.com/CarlaNecoleWilliams
https://twitter.com/carlanecolemba

About the Author

Carla Necole Williams is fiercely committed to guiding men and women who are on a quest for personal fulfillment to free themselves from past shackles by healing their inner child, be empowered by learning to love, value and appreciate themselves and elevate their emotional intelligence and raise their spiritual awareness in order to deliberately create the life they want.

With six years of experience working with amazing clients with similar worries and concerns and guiding them to achieve remarkable success, her mission and commitment is to provide a safe space for her clients to heal, love and empower yourself.

Her path to become an Inner Healing Coach became clear as she set out to heal her own hurts, pains and disappointments. As a child she daydreamed about becoming a pediatrician because she always wanted to help and heal hurting children. Turns out, coaching not medicine, is her calling; however, her purpose is still the same: To help and heal the inner child.

Bibliography

Anthony, Robert. *The secret of doing without doing.* 1 Apr. 2015. <http://www.abundance-and-happiness.com/robert-anthony-the-secret-of-doing-without-doing.html>

Ford, Deborah. (2010). *The Dark Side of the Light Chasers.* New York, NY: Riverhead Books.

Schwartz, Robert. (2010). *Your Soul's Plan: Discovering the Real Meaning of the Life You Planned Before You Were Born.* Berkeley, CA: North Atlantic Books.

Tolle, Eckhart. (2010) *The Power of Now: A Guide to Spiritual Enlightenment.* Novato, CA: New World Library.

Walsch, Neale Donald. (1997). *Conversations with God: Bk. 1: An Uncommon Dialogue.* Hachette, UK: Hodder & Stoughton.

44416922R00084

Made in the USA
Charleston, SC
23 July 2015